I

EVERYDAY
AMERICAN HISTORY OF THE 20TH CENTURY

EVERYDAY

AMERICAN HISTORY OF THE 20TH CENTURY

FROM THE RECONSTRUCTION TO THE PRESENT DAY

BY RICHARD RUBIN

A Byron Preiss Book

Doubleday Direct, Inc
Garden City, New York

Copyright © 1998 by Byron Preiss Visual Publications, Inc.
Photo credits: © 1998 Archive Holdings—5, 10, 21, 31, 32, 56, 66, 67, 94, 96, 98, 101, 104, 115, 160, 167, 177, 191, 193, 195, 205, 209, 213, 216. © 1998 AP World Wide—44, 62, 72, 77, 145, 211. © 1998 Bureau of Engraving and Printing—9, 29, 29, 43, 112, 198, 201, 204, 206, 217. © 1998 Bettman—25, 37, 46, 55, 74, 78, 86, 102, 123, 127, 130, 175, 181, 188. © 1998 Dwight Eisenhower Library—186. © 1998 Franklin Deleanor Roosevelt Library—129. © 1998 National Archives—7, 153, 158, 169, 182.

Published by GuildAmerica™ Books,
an imprint and trademark registration pending of Doubleday Direct, Inc.,
Department GB, 401 Franklin Avenue, Garden City, New York 11430

ISBN: 1-56865-776-5

Cover design by Steven Jablonoski

10 9 8 7 6 5 4 3 2 1

First Edition: 1998

CONTENTS

INTRODUCTION

W hat, exactly, comes to mind when you hear the word "history"? Be honest, now. If you're like most people, those three syllables summon up one of two things: either the notion of a past so remote as to be irrelevant (as in the expression "that's history!") or a vague memory of having to memorize long lists of names and dates, the kind of recollection that can still make you shudder. Perhaps you're wincing, thinking about all the history you've forgotten, but it's a safe bet that you know more history—especially modern American history—than you realize. You probably know something about Theodore Roosevelt and Woodrow Wilson and Franklin Delano Roosevelt, about the Wild West and the Roaring Twenties and the Great Depression, about the Spanish-American War and the First World War and the Second World War. It's just that, well, you're not quite sure how much you remember, and how much you think you might remember, and who and what came first, and when and where exactly. For some reason, dates like 1881 and 1898 and 1912 and 1933 and 1948 stick in your mind, and names and phrases like Charles Guiteau and Eugene V. Debs and the Bull Moose Party and the Teapot Dome Scandal ring a bell, but you're not quite sure why. Maybe you even want to find out, to remember what you forgot from those old history classes and perhaps learn a little more while you're at it. But the thought of cracking open those old textbooks . . . not too appealing, is it?

The problem is that too many of those old textbooks aren't much more than lists of names and dates, those same lists that can still make you break out in a cold sweat just thinking about them. The bad news is: those old history textbooks and classes might have been tedious experiences that have turned you off to the subject. The good news is: history is anything *but* a dry list of names and dates. In truth, history is—as you might guess from the word itself—a story. To be a bit more precise, history is a massive web of stories, some of which follow or precede other stories, some of which explain other stories, and some of which have nothing to do with any other stories but are worth telling, and listening to, just because they're so interesting. They are stories about ambition and greed and jealousy and pride and honor and idealism and risk and reward and failure and genius and stupidity and hatred and love. Above all, they are stories about people—people who faced situations we encounter every day, and people who had experiences that were absolutely unique.

History is not fixed, not two-dimensional, not black-and-white; it is always open to interpretation, always subject to speculation, always riddled with mystery. Only one thing is certain about history: All of it was essential to creating the world we live in today. In that regard, every story you will read in this book, and any other history book, is *your* story, too. What happens to you today has a great deal to do with what happened to other people a century ago; what you do tomorrow is influenced, whether you know it or not, by what other people did yesterday. In learning about history, we invariably learn a lot about ourselves, too.

This book deals with American history since 1880—a period when the United States was transformed from a relatively small, remote, and isolated outpost to the planet's richest, most powerful, and most influential nation. It is also, not coincidentally, a period that produced some of the world's most unforgettable characters—and some of its best stories.

CHAPTER 1

THE OLD CENTURY

U.S. POPULATION:
50,155,783 (1880)
62,622,250 (1890)

OH, WHERE DO WE BEGIN?

To understand America in 1880, you have to understand that it really wasn't America at all, at least not America in the sense that we think of it today. Sure, if you were somehow to find your way into a time machine and travel back to 1880, you'd probably be able to make your way around. After all, the language hasn't changed, at least not entirely. But what, exactly, would you see? More important, what *wouldn't* you see?

Well, of course, you wouldn't see automobiles or airplanes or subways, and you wouldn't see telephones or phonographs or electric lights or electric anything unless

1

you were in a scientific laboratory or a public facility (like a government building or a police station) or a tiny handful of very affluent and progress-oriented households (and you probably wouldn't be able to actually *call* anyone, anyway, since no one *else* had a telephone).

If you came across a group of children or adults engaged in some sort of sporting event, it would almost certainly be baseball or some variation on that game; football was played in few places, hockey was only played north of the border, and basketball hadn't even been invented yet. You almost certainly wouldn't see any building taller than three stories, unless you were in a large city, where you might see some as tall as five stories. You'd have to make a special trip to a department store or some other large commercial or industrial facility to see an elevator or escalator.

You wouldn't see huge, sprawling cities. You wouldn't see suburbs. You wouldn't see massive, industrial-scale farms. You wouldn't see powerful labor unions or a minimum wage or a maximum work week or child-labor laws. You wouldn't see an income tax or an election for U.S. Senator (both institutions—income tax and the direct election of U.S. Senators—were not established nationally until 1913).

Come to think of it, chances are you wouldn't see a female voter—or a black voter, either, not even in states that had abolished slavery long before the Civil War. You probably wouldn't see anyone who wasn't of British, Scottish, Irish, German, or African descent, unless you were in the Midwest, which had a large, recently arrived Scandinavian population, or in San Francisco, which had a sizable Chinese community (although you probably wouldn't see a Chinese voter).

You wouldn't see much in terms of quality health care or public aid or safety codes or government regulations on food, drugs, housing, or business practices. In many parts of the country—most parts, really—you wouldn't see an awful lot of indoor plumbing.

You *would* see a majority of citizens living on farms or in small towns. You'd see a country that was largely agricultural, largely conservative, relatively homogenous, relatively small in population (especially given its huge area), still existing in the shadow of the great European empires, still centered along the eastern seaboard, still very much in the grip of the Civil War, even though it had been over for fifteen years.

You'd see a country that was still very much in its youth, still inexperienced in matters of foreign intrigue and international finance and literature and the arts. You'd see a country that had a sure sense of its own magnificent destiny and its eventual paramount position in the world, but which still had a great distance to go before it would realize that destiny, and assume that paramount position. In other words, a totally different America from the one we know today. And yet, that America was really not that far off.

Within a decade, the face of the country—who lived in America and where—would change entirely. Within two decades, America would defeat a major world power in a war and become an imperial power in its own right. Within four, it would be credited with determining the outcome of the greatest war the planet had ever seen, one that had consumed the entire globe for four long years. Within seven, it would be the richest, most powerful nation in the history of the world.

SOME MIGHTY UGLY BUSINESS

After the Civil War, the U.S. Government and the U.S. Army turned its attention out West, determined to clear the way for white settlement throughout what would eventually become the continental United States. "Clearing the way" meant, to a large extent, clearing the Native Americans, or Indians, out. By 1880, following some messy battles, like the famous one at Little Bighorn in 1876, the way was pretty much "cleared." (The reason Little Big Horn is remembered today—aside from the fact that it was "Custer's Last Stand"—is that it was one of the few times the Native Americans actually won a lopsided victory against the U.S. Army. For the most part, the cavalry massacred the Indians, who, in many cases, were unarmed women and children.) By the late 1870s, the U.S. Army managed to defeat some proud and revered old tribes in the mid- north- and southwest, including the Apache, Cheyenne, Modoc, Arapaho, Paiute, and Ute. And then there were the Nez Perce, an Oregon-based tribe whose chief, Joseph, led the tattered remnants of his nation on a 1,700-mile trek toward the Canadian border for refuge, winning several battles before finally being stopped by U.S. General Nelson Miles. On October 5, 1877, Chief Joseph surrendered, declaring:

"I am tired of fighting. Our chiefs are killed. . . . The old men are all killed. . . . It is cold and we have no blankets. The little children are freezing to death. My people, some of them, have run away to the hills, and have no blankets, no food; no one knows where they are, perhaps freezing to death. I want time to look for my children and see how many of them I can find. Maybe I shall find them among

SOME MIGHTY UGLY BUSINESS (*continued*)

the dead. Hear me, my chiefs, I am tired; my heart is sick and sad. From where the sun now stands, I will fight no more forever."

Chief Joseph

Chief Joseph and the surviving Nez Perces were sent to reservations in Oklahoma.

The most formidable Indian tribe, however—at least from the perspective of the U.S. Cavalry—was the Sioux. It was the Sioux who had defeated Custer at Little Big Horn, the Sioux who had produced the charismatic leaders Crazy Horse and Sitting Bull, and the Sioux who made their home in the Black Hills of South Dakota, an area they considered sacred and was rumored to contain gold. That last fact made it just a matter of time before the

SOME MIGHTY UGLY BUSINESS (*continued*)

Sioux, too, were confined to a reservation, their sacred turf opened up to white settlement. By 1881, the U.S. Army had prevailed in Dakota: Crazy House was dead and Sitting Bull had returned from self-imposed Canadian exile, surrendering as a prisoner of war. Two years later, he was released from prison and relocated to the Standing Rock reservation in South Dakota. In 1885, he traveled with "Buffalo" Bill Cody's Wild West Show.

A few years later, on a Paiute reservation in Nevada, a Native American calling himself Wovoka underwent a religious experience and started preaching a new religion based upon the belief that an Indian Messiah was about to arrive who would return North America to the indigenous people and reunite them with their deceased relatives and ancestors (and in the process, revive the exterminated buffalo, a staple of Indian life). The centerpiece of Wovoka's new religion was the Ghost Dance, a mystical, charismatic exercise that helped spread the religion to other reservations across the West very quickly. Naturally, this alarmed some folks in the U.S. government, who sent the army out to suppress the new religion. New attention was focused on the Sioux, who were seen as a "hotbed" of Ghost Dancing, and on Sitting Bull, who refused to stop Ghost Dancing at Standing Rock Reservation. On December 15, 1890, the government sent Indian police to arrest Sitting Bull outside his cabin on the reservation. When some Ghost Dancers attempted to rescue Sitting Bull, the Indian police started shooting. Sitting Bull was hit and killed.

Two weeks later, the U.S. Seventh Cavalry were searching some 350 Sioux prisoners (230 of them were women and children) at Wounded Knee Creek when someone discovered a rifle and a shot was fired. What ensued was a slaughter. In a matter of minutes, approximately half the Indians had been kill or mor-

SOME MIGHTY UGLY BUSINESS (*continued*)

Sitting Bull

SOME MIGHTY UGLY BUSINESS (*continued*)

tally wounded. Twenty-four soldiers were killed, too, most by friendly fire. The massacre, remembered today as the Battle of Wounded Knee, was the last "battle" of the "Indian Wars."

Quite a change. And, though few—if any—Americans realized it at the time, that change began in earnest around 1880. And like most major transformations, America's may, indeed, have started with a bang. Well, maybe two bangs.

IT'S 1881. DUCK!

On March 1, 1881, Czar Alexander II of Russia was riding in a carriage through the streets of St. Petersburg when someone threw a bomb at him, killing him. This occurrence, some five thousand miles from American shores, would soon have a profound and lasting impact upon the United States. But first, let's deal with the second bang, which would happen a little closer to home—and exactly four months and one day later.

July 2, 1881: James A. Garfield, a Republican who had defeated Civil War hero Winfield Scott Hancock in the presidential election of 1880, was standing on the platform of the Baltimore and Potomac Railroad station in Washington, D.C., waiting to catch a train to Massachusetts for the July Fourth holiday. Garfield, the last president to actually be born in a log cabin, had been a professor of Greek and Latin, a college president, a minister, a general in the Union Army, a congressman from Ohio, and a real party politician. What kind of president

President James A. Garfield

was Garfield? Well, that's kind of hard to tell: As of July 2, 1881, he had only held the office for 120 days. Not much time to get anything done, especially in those days, before air travel and the proliferation of instantaneous communication.

It was time enough, though, to offend thirty-nine-year-old Charles J. Guiteau. Actually, Garfield didn't have to do much of anything to offend the man. Guiteau, as they say, wasn't quite right in the head. He frequently claimed to be either "an agent of God" and "premier of England" (never mind that England has never had a premier). He also claimed to be a Republican "stalwart" who was entitled to the job of U.S. Consul in Paris for having supported Garfield in the election. When the president failed to give him his "rightful" position, Guiteau took matters into his own hands.

Slipping out of the station's men's room, Guiteau

President Chester A. Arthur

stepped up onto the platform, pulled a British bulldog gun out of his pocket and shot Garfield twice in the back. "I am a stalwart and Arthur shall be president!" Guiteau shouted. "My God! What is that?" Garfield cried as he fell. The president lingered for eighty days; for a while, in August, it seemed as if he might recover. But then his condition deteriorated and on September 19, 1881, James A. Garfield died.

Guiteau was right: Garfield's vice president, Chester A. Arthur, did become president. But Arthur didn't make Guiteau consul to Paris either. Instead, the assassin was tried for murder, convicted, and, though he was clearly insane, sentenced to death. On June 30, 1882, some 4,000 spectators assembled to witness the hanging. Guiteau, ascending to the gallows, sang, "I am going to the Lordy, I am so glad." A few minutes later he was dead.

It was the second presidential assassination in U.S. history, and it would not be the last. Unlike the others, Lincoln in 1865, and two more yet to come in the twentieth century, Garfield's assassination can hardly be considered a political act, and, unlike the other three, it did not really carry political repercussions. But the country's first presidential assassination—of Abraham Lincoln, just sixteen years earlier—had been viewed, largely, as an isolated incident, the last tragic act of a tragic civil war. With the assassination of President Garfield, it grew more and more apparent that America was, indeed, becoming a different country, one in which violence would increasingly shape the course of history. Call it a loss of innocence or a wake-up call placed by modern reality or just another senseless killing. Whatever it was, it changed the country forever, even if no one would so much as begin to realize it for a couple more decades.

OK, NOW, BACK TO RUSSIA

One of the wonderful things about studying history is that you encounter fascinating little ironies almost everywhere you look. Take the assassination of Czar Alexander II. He was blown up, as it were, by leftists who were sick and tired of a monarchy and a country that was mired in the sixteenth century, a nation where the vast majority of the population was dirt poor and had few, if any, basic civil rights. The irony is that Alexander II, who was sixty-two years old and had reigned for twenty-six years, was actually starting to bring about some reforms; he had even taken steps to emancipate Russia's serfs, who lived and worked in virtual slavery. He was just doing it all very slowly—too slowly for more progressive Russians, who still saw him as a bad guy.

He was not nearly as bad, though—in another of those historical ironies—as the guy who replaced him, who happened to be the late czar's thirty-six-year-old son, Alexander III. Immediately after his father's assassination, Alexander III, who had always sat somewhat to the right of his father, began a reign of terror against the usual Russian scapegoats: leftists, Roman Catholics, and, especially, Jews. His new policy decreed that one-third will convert, one-third will leave, and one-third will die. Those who would leave—Jews, leftists, Roman Catholics, and the perennially poor who just couldn't take it anymore—started to do so almost immediately. They left from almost every part of the vast Russian empire, which, in those days, included Lithuania, Latvia, Estonia, Belarus (Byelorussia), Ukraine, Moldova, and much of what is now Poland. As the tide of eastern European emigration snowballed, it quickly spread down south, to Hungary and Czechoslovakia (then part of the Austro-Hungarian Empire; today known as the Czech Republic and Slovakia), Romania, Italy, the Balkan States (known today as the former Yugoslavia; if you're confused, you're not alone), and Greece.

Some went to Germany or France or England. Some journeyed across the Atlantic to Canada and Mexico and Central America and South America. But for the overwhelming majority, the destination of choice was—you guessed it—the United States of America. How many? Well, between 1881 and 1890 alone, 5,246,613, to be exact. In other words, the equivalent of 10.46 percent of America's population at the beginning of that decade. In today's terms, that would mean that approximately

28 million immigrants would arrive here over the next ten years.

Why did they come? For many, the lure was the promise of freedom of speech, freedom of religion, freedom of expression, freedom of thought itself. For others, the motivation was somewhat more pragmatic: slowly starving to death in Europe, unable to own land or their own business or earn a decent wage or break free from a rigid caste system, they had little to lose. They might not have believed the legend that American streets were paved with gold, but they did believe in America as the Land of Opportunity, where they could, potentially, rise as far as their ambition and intelligence could take them, unfettered by a humble birth or ethnic prejudice. And if this didn't always prove to be the case, at least they were better off than they had been back in the old country. At least they could expect to make some kind of a living here. And many came with no greater expectation than to work, save up some money, and eventually return back home, which they did.

Many, many more, though, stayed. They married, raised families, learned English, and slowly rose up the economic ladder. From an overcrowded tenement apartment in an overcrowded slum, they aspired to a slightly less crowded apartment in a less crowded, better-kept neighborhood, and from there, eventually to their own homes. Often the journey would take a generation, sometimes two or three. But few immigrants actually ended up worse off for having immigrated. For the most part, the journey and upheaval paid off, if only slowly and slightly.

The immigrants arrived at the ports of Boston and Philadelphia and Baltimore and Galveston, but the most popular destination was New York. Some left immediately, joining relatives who had emigrated before them; others struck out for rural communities and semi-utopian colonies that they'd heard of only by hearsay and reputation, and some became itinerant peddlers and craftsmen. Most, though, either stayed in the city at which they had arrived (again, for the most part, New York) or settled in another major American city, further inland; Chicago, St. Louis, Detroit, Milwaukee, and Cleveland were among the most popular secondary destinations.

Why cities? The two most common reasons were family (or community) and, even more important, jobs. In fact, chances were the family and community were also there for the jobs. Generally speaking, employment opportunities in small towns and rural areas were extremely limited (the major exception was rural coal mines, which employed large numbers of southern and eastern European immigrants), but, with the advent of the Industrial Revolution, cities had become centers of manufacturing. A typical midsize American city would have a few large factories, mills, and plants, each of which employed hundreds or even thousands of unskilled laborers. A large city might have dozens of such factories and plants, even more. It was all the product of a vicious cycle: Manufacturers built their factories in cities on the premise that the large local population would furnish an ample labor pool that would work for low wages because of the inherent competition; hearing that there were jobs to be had in a particular city, unemployed Americans and recent immigrants would flock there in search of work, increasing the size of the labor pool, which would, in turn, attract more manufacturers. The work, by and large, was unpleasant, usually monotonous, often physically taxing, occasionally dangerous. Workers were expected to work long hours for wages that were, in many cases, subsistence level. Often, workers were paid not by the hour but by some arbitrary measure of their productivity (there's a good reason that garment factories, for example, were known as sweatshops). Still, typically the work was steady and didn't require a knowledge of English, and so it naturally appealed to immigrants.

STATE YOUR NAME, PLEASE

Between 1876 and 1889, there were thirty-eight states in America. By 1896, there were forty-five; four had been added in one month alone (who says Congress never gets anything done?). All the additions were made, not surprisingly, out West. They included:

North Dakota, November 2, 1889;
South Dakota, November 2, 1889;
Montana, November 8, 1889;
Washington, November 11, 1889;
Idaho, July 3, 1890;
Wyoming, July 10, 1890;
Utah, January 4, 1896.

In the two decades before the turn of the century, the imbalance that had always existed between rural America (where a majority of Americans lived) and urban America was reversing itself at a rapid pace. Not until 1920 would more Americans live in cities than in small towns or out in the country, but between 1880 and 1900, the typical U.S. city expanded dramatically, both in population and in area, often doubling or tripling in size. Cities themselves competed with each other to draw both foreign immigrants and domestic emigrants, building opera houses and theaters, libraries and museums, public schools and universities, parks and beaches, sophisticated sewage and mass-transit systems, public stadiums and professional baseball teams. And even if most of the people who moved to the cities could only rarely take advantage of such perks they were attractive draws, just one more factor in the explosive growth of U.S. cities before the turn of the century.

MEANWHILE, BACK AT THE RANCH . . .

Wait a minute, you're saying. What's all this talk about cities? Wasn't this the heyday of the Wild West? Well, just hold your horses (sorry, I couldn't resist). True, the time and place that we think of as the "Wild West"— cowboys and Indians, sheriffs and outlaws, the Chisholm Trail and the shoot-out at the O.K. Corral—did, in fact, largely occur in the last quarter of the nineteenth century. But it's also true that the "winning" of the West had begun well before the Civil War, and that, by 1880, the West wasn't really all that "wild" anymore, at least not in the way we think of it.

For one thing, the "Indian Wars," as they were known, were mostly over by 1880, the American Indians having lost—lost, in many cases, their land, their identity, their heritage, their lives—and been, for the most part, relocated to squalid, cramped reservations, often thousands of miles away from their native territory.

Contrary to the popular image, many Western towns, if not most, banned firearms or alcoholic beverages or both. The most valuable asset to any community wasn't oil or livestock or even gold; it was water, without which nothing else could exist. The typical Western denizen wasn't a taciturn loner, but a member of a family of small homesteaders. The typical occupation wasn't lawman or cowboy, but rancher and ranch-hand, storekeeper, and railroad worker. And the typical "cowboy" was just that—a cattle tender who made his living driving large herds to market, a journey that might take weeks or even months.

True, cowboys did wear ten-gallon hats to protect them from the sun and kerchiefs to protect them from trail dust. True, they were typically handy with a lariat and often carried a six-shooter, mostly to protect their herd from rustlers, poachers, and wild animals (although they might also need to protect themselves from irate landowners or Native Americans, as well, since trespassing was an unavoidable part of driving cattle to market). But cowboys weren't all loners, nor were they all white Americans; there were Chinese and Mexican and European cowboys, and, according to some estimates, at least one cowboy in four was African-American, many of them recently emancipated from slavery.

If cowboys were a diverse lot, they were, in that respect, no different than the rest of Western society. Homesteading—the program by which the government literally gave away land to anyone who was willing to live on it for a certain amount of time—drew a broad spectrum of people westward, everyone from old-line Southerners and New England Yankees to emancipated slaves to Chinese, Scandinavian, German, Jewish, Irish, Italian and Eastern European immigrants fresh off the boat. The West, in its own way, was as much of a melting pot as the inner city, except that, instead of crowding into tenements, the immigrants who went West often ended up with too much living space—so much that they often had to ride for hours in order to see human beings other than the ones they lived with.

Despite the fact that the "Wild West" was hardly as wild or exciting as we may have been led to believe, the people who settled and worked the land did, no doubt, live through the kind of experiences that inspired legends and, ultimately, an entire genre of books and movies, starting with the publication of Owen Wister's novel *The Virginian* in 1902. If you're looking to discover what "won" the West, though, there are three answers, not one being as glamorous as a pearl-handled Colt six-shooter or a gold-plated, six-pointed sheriff's star: *irrigation*, which made ranching and homesteading possible in areas where water was often scarce; *barbed wire*, which enabled cattle ranchers to raise huge herds on ample grazing land without worrying about them wandering off; the *railroad*, which brought settlers, supplies, jobs, and mail. Railroads, in fact, were utterly essential all over the country, from Nevada to New York. They moved people, cattle, and all kinds of goods around and made it possible to travel from one coast to another without undertaking an overlong voyage by ship or a dangerous one by stagecoach. Railroads made the concept of a single, undivided, universally accessible America a reality.

They also made a handful of men very, very rich. And, in that way, too, they helped define the era.

OLIGARCHS AND ORGANIZERS

History now remembers them as "robber barons," a handful of extremely rich and extremely powerful men who dominated the U.S. economy—and, to a certain extent, America itself—in the 1880s and 1890s. They made their fortunes either in some industry itself or by financing industries. They crushed their competitors, built unbreakable monopolies or "trusts," imported boatloads of immigrants for cheap labor (69 percent of Slovakian men in America back then worked as coal miners), in most cases paid their workers poorly, in all cases lived lavishly (so lavishly that the era is now remembered as "the Gilded Age"), and generally had little regard for public opinion. Most of all, they thrived in an era of unprecedented greed and ambition, supported by presidential administrations more friendly to Big Business than any in U.S. history. There was Andrew Carnegie, the Scottish immigrant who had built a massive empire on steel, then expanded into iron and even coal, which he needed to fuel his furnaces; John D. Rockefeller, who turned a small oil refinery in Cleveland into Standard Oil, which by 1880 controlled 90 percent of all the oil in America; J. Pierpont Morgan, the banker who would eventually help create U.S. Steel, the largest corporation in the world; and the "railroad barons," including Jay Gould and William Vanderbilt, who between them had cornered a large percentage of the nation's railways, owning everything from tracks and depots to steel mills to make their trains and coal mines to power them.

Some of the robber barons, most notably Carnegie and Rockefeller, dedicated a great deal of their time and energy to giving away vast sums of money, but in general, public opinion of them and their peers was rather low. They were perceived and caricatured as greedy, ruthless, selfish, opulent, ostentatious, insensitive, mean-spirited, and crude—and, truth be told, they often were. They were also, in most cases, unconcerned with their public image. "The public be damned," Vanderbilt once said, and most of his peers, it seemed, were inclined to agree with him. After all, what could the public really do to them?

For the most part, nothing, because the "little people" needed the work and couldn't afford to complain. But in the 1880s and 1890s, that, too, was starting to change.

Back in 1869, a group of tailors in Philadelphia formed a secret mutual-support society and named it, somewhat optimistically, the Knights of Labor. The group grew slowly but steadily. In 1877, a bitter railroad strike, instigated by two pay cuts within a single year, spread across the country and galvanized broad support for labor. The strikes were eventually put down by federal troops, but labor organizers realized a boon, and by 1885 the Knights of Labor had 110,000 members.

The following year, they joined with the Federation of Organized Trades and Labor Unions to form the American Federation of Labor, or AFL. That same year, 1886, there were some 1,500 strikes across America. One of them, which started in Chicago on May 1, was a loosely organized attempt to bring about an eight-hour workday. Two days later, when the strikers picketed the McCormick Harvesting Machine Company, police fired into the crowd, killing four people. The next day, strikers and anarchists organized a rally in Chicago's Haymarket to protest the killings. When police moved in to break up the crowd, someone threw a bomb at them; one policeman was killed instantly, and seven more later died of their injuries. The police fired wildly into the crowd, killing another seven or eight people, and injuring about a hundred more, many of them fellow policemen. "For-

Haymarket Riot—1886

eigners" were blamed for the violence, and eight men—
seven of them German, all of them anarchists—were arrested. They were all convicted of conspiracy, and the
following year four were hanged; a fifth hanged himself
in his jail cell the night before the state was scheduled
execute him. Six years later, the governor of Illinois,
forty-five-year-old John Peter Altgeld (himself a German-
American), pardoned the three survivors, an act that may
have ended his political career.

The Haymarket Affair, as it is now known, triggered a
widespread wave of fear and distrust toward foreigners,
political leftists, labor organizers, and unions. Neverthe-

less, unions persevered, drawing members from railroad
workers, coal miners, and other industrial laborers. One
of the largest contributors were the massive steel mills
in and around Pittsburgh, and one of the largest of those
was Andrew Carnegie's mill in Homestead, Pennsylvania.
In 1889, workers at the mill—many of whom were members of the Amalgamated Association of Iron and Steel
Workers, the country's most powerful trade union—
struck for higher pay and better working conditions.
They won a three-year contract with favorable terms.
When the contract came up for renewal, though, in
1892, Carnegie decided to break the union. Carnegie
had his plant manager, Henry Clay Frick, increase production quotas, anticipating that the new demands
would trigger a strike. When Carnegie's prediction came
to pass, he had Frick lock the striking steelworkers out
of the plant, then fired them on July 2. Strikers continued to picket the plant, and took control of the town of
Homestead itself, which was largely owned by the company and occupied entirely by steelworkers.

Frick contacted the Pinkerton Company and had them
send three hundred armed guards. They arrived by
barge in Homestead on July 6 and were met at the dock
by ten thousand strikers. In the battle that ensued, seven
of the Pinkertons were killed (along with nine of the
strikers), and most of the rest were injured before they
surrendered. Six days later, Pennsylvania's governor sent
eight thousand state militia troops to protect the plant
and the replacement workers Frick had hired.

On July 23, a twenty-two-year-old Russian-born anarchist named Alexander Berkman charged into Frick's office, shot the plant manager, then stabbed Frick several
times before being subdued by bodyguards. While Frick

was not critically hurt (he only missed a week of work) the act dulled public support for the strikers (Berkman was sentenced to fourteen years in prison and was deported after World War I), and the plant began arresting strikers on trumped-up charges that diverted attention from the strike and taxed the union's financial resources.

Unable to interrupt the plant or even maintain the strike, the strikers capitulated on November 20. Carnegie, having broken the union, lowered wages and increased working hours. But his relationship with Frick, the right-hand man whom Carnegie had set up as the "villain" of the strike, was ruined. Years later, after they had stopped speaking altogether, Carnegie called on Frick at his Fifth Avenue mansion. Frick refused to see Carnegie, ordering his butler only to pass on the message: "Tell him I'll see him in hell, where we're both going."

The Homestead Strike was, in the end, a failure. Deplorable working conditions were exacerbated, many strikers lost their jobs permanently, and the union was virtually destroyed. But the strike—and the strikers—also captured the country's attention and focused it on the cause of organized labor. It would be forty years before trade unions would enjoy any kind of real sustained success and power in America, but from 1892 on, Americans knew they were out there, and many were sympathetic to their cause.

"A SPLENDID LITTLE WAR"

The Haymarket Affair, the Homestead Strike, and other labor-industry clashes of the 1880s and 1890s were a mixcd bag for both bosses and workers, not to mention ordinary Americans, who saw coal and steel prices rise and fall and railroad service disrupted with every strike. In the end, it seemed, nobody came away from the era's big strikes a true winner—nobody, that is, except for the publishers of America's newspapers, for whom all news was good news.

It was the era of "yellow" (or sensationalist) journalism, of tabloids with headlines in bold four-inch type, and two publishers reigned supreme: Hungarian-born Joseph Pulitzer, owner of the *St. Louis Post-Dispatch* and *The New York World,* and William Randolph Hearst, who owned *The San Francisco Examiner* and *The New York Journal.* Both Hearst and Pulitzer used their papers to wage war on corruption and graft and anyone they disliked; both hired large staffs of investigative journalists—"muckrakers"—to expose scandal and wrongdoing. And each had his own pet causes.

Both Hearst and Pulitzer, for example, had a soft spot for the insurgents who were fighting autocratic Spanish rule on the island of Cuba. Pulitzer enlisted Cuban insurgents as correspondents; Hearst sent the artist Frederick Remington to sketch battles even though no war had been declared, promising Remington: "You furnish the pictures and I'll furnish the war." With their graphic descriptions of Spain's ruthless war against the insurgents, Hearst and Pulitzer stirred up a great deal of public sentiment against Spain.

But not enough for a war. Even when the battleship U.S.S. *Maine* exploded in Havana harbor on February 15, 1898, killing 260 American sailors—and setting off rumors that it had been sunk by a Spanish mine—President William McKinley hesitated to declare war.

HEARST, THE WIZARD OF OOZE

Hearst as a scarecrow rising from a pool of mud appeared   ran for Governor of New York. Rival newspapers beat
in *Harper's Weekly* in 1906, when the yellow publisher   him by exposing his "plundering deals" in Wall Street.

*Hearst as a scarecrow rising from a pool of mud
—Harper's Weekly 1906*

(Decades later, experts determined that the explosion
that sank the *Maine* had actually occurred inside the
ship.) Ten days later, the Assistant Secretary of the
U.S. Navy, a forty-year-old New Yorker named Theo-

dore Roosevelt, ordered Admiral George Dewey to sail his Pacific Fleet to Hong Kong and prepare to attack the Spanish fleet in Manila Bay should war be declared, as Roosevelt eagerly hoped it would.

Roosevelt did not, in fact, have the authority to issue such an order, and the action itself actually brought the United States closer to war by helping to force McKinley's hesitant hand. Spain, meanwhile, accommodated the United States by offering to negotiate independence for Cuba.

By now, though, it was too late; too many powerful people in Congress and McKinley's administration were anxious for war, including many former Confederates (among them former C.S.A. General Fitzhugh Lee, the U.S. Consul in Havana), who believed that a foreign war would serve to erase lingering tensions between the North and the South, while McKinley feared that a lack of war with Spain would, in fact, hurt the Republican party and his own chances for re-election. He and Congress demanded that Spain grant Cuba independence immediately. Spain, affronted, broke off diplomatic relations with the United States on April 21, 1898, and, three days later, declared war.

McKinley called for 125,000 volunteers. Among the most notable men to answer McKinley's call were Theodore Roosevelt (who offered to raise his own cavalry unit, "Roosevelt's Rough Riders") and former Confederate General Joe Wheeler. (During a battle near Santiago, Cuba, several months later, Wheeler drove a Spanish unit into retreat and shouted to his men: "We've got the damn Yankees on the run!") Things moved quickly from there.

On May 1, Admiral Dewey's Asiatic Squadron steamed

into Manila Bay to attack the Spanish fleet. Spanish Admiral Montojo, a genuinely chivalrous nineteenth-century type, sailed his fleet out of the harbor and into the bay so that no civilians might be hurt. Despite this noble gesture, Dewey showed him no mercy. Within hours, every ship in the antiquated, outgunned, ill-trained Spanish fleet had been destroyed with 381 Spanish sailors killed; not a single U.S. ship was damaged, not a single U.S. sailor killed. It was a bad sign for Spain.

Ten days later, U.S. Marines landed at Guantanamo Bay, Cuba. Soon 17,000 U.S. troops were on their way to the island and, by June 24, had won their first battle, at Las Guasimas. On July 1, Roosevelt's Rough Riders, accompanied by two regiments of African-American troops, made their famous charge up San Juan Hill, taking it at the cost of some 1,500 U.S. casualties. Two days later, the U.S. Navy destroyed the Spanish fleet in Santiago Harbor, at a cost of two U.S. casualties. By July 17, U.S. troops had taken the city of Santiago after the hottest fighting of the war. The cost: some 1,700 U.S. casualties. By the twenty-fifth, the United States had taken the city of Guanica, Puerto Rico, without much trouble at all.

By July 26, Spain was suing for peace.

When it was all over, Secretary of State John Hay told Theodore Roosevelt that it had been a "splendid little war." How little? In all, 379 U.S. servicemen had been killed in battle; some 5,000 more had died of disease. Small when compared with the more recent Civil War, which had claimed 600,000 lives. "Little," indeed, when you consider that, in less than four months, the United States had routed a major world power, liberated Cuba from Spanish control, taken control of Puerto Rico and the Philippines, and announced to the world that it was going to be a major power in the twentieth century.

THE FORGETTABLE PRESIDENTS?

Maybe it's not a nice thing to say, but here it is: Between 1881 and 1897, the United States had five presidents, and not one of them was particularly memorable. None could be classified as a "great" chief executive, none said or did anything truly exceptional, and, to tell the truth, none even looked very interesting. Well, there it is. Still, they were presidents, and they do deserve a little extra attention. After all, as schoolchildren, we're all required, at one time or another, to memorize their names, or at least try (thank heavens the same doesn't hold true for vice presidents). Some day, your child or grandchild may even come to you and ask you about them. What do you do then? How do you remember these forgettable presidents? Here are some tips:

James Abram Garfield (1831–1881): Served March 4 to September 19, 1881. Fluent in both Latin and Greek, and could write one language with his left hand and the other with his right—simultaneously. His mother lived with him and his wife, Lucretia, in the White House. Second president to be assassinated.

Chester Alan Arthur (1830–1886): Served September 19, 1881, to March 4, 1885. Two different towns in Vermont claim to be his birthplace, but he may, in fact, have been born in Canada (which, if true, would have made him ineligible for the presidency). Crony of legendarily corrupt New York political boss Roscoe Conkling, yet proved to be surprisingly honest once president. Refused to move into the White House until twenty-four wagon-loads of "junk"—including a bag belonging to Abigail Adams, a

THE FORGETTABLE PRESIDENTS? (*continued*)

hat worn by John Quincy Adams, and a pair of Lincoln's trousers—had been cleaned out and sold at auction.

President Grover Cleveland

Grover Cleveland (1837–1908): Served March 4, 1885, to March 4, 1889, and March 4, 1893, to March 4, 1897. Paid a substitute to fight for him in the Civil War because he was his elderly mother's only means of support. Former sheriff of Erie County, New York. Between 1880 and 1884 was elected mayor of Buffalo, governor of New York, and president. Rumored to have fathered an out-of-wedlock child in Buffalo, leading supporters of his opponent in the 1884 election, James G. Blaine, to chant: "Ma, Ma, where's my Pa? Gone to the White House, ha-ha-ha!" Married his twenty-three-year-old ward, Frances Folsom, during his first term in the White House. Only man ever to serve two non-consecutive terms as president; only Democratic president between James Buchanan and Woodrow Wilson. Notoriously honest, incorruptible, and blunt.

President Benjamin Harrison

Benjamin Harrison (1833–1901): Served March 4, 1889, to March 4, 1893. Grandson of President William Henry ("Tippecanoe") Harrison, the only grandson of a president to be elected to the office himself. Five-foot-six-inches tall. During the Civil War, rose in rank from lieutenant to general. Taught a men's Bible class. Served one term as senator from Indiana; ran, unsuccessfully, for governor twice. Widowed near the end of his term, he later married his wife's niece. Installed electricity in the White House but was afraid to turn the light switch on or off.

Of course, it didn't seem little at all to the thousands of soldiers who came home injured or maimed, or to the many thousands who lost a loved one to Spanish gunfire or some tropical illness. But even to them, the Spanish-American War would seem "little," even quaint, when compared to what lay ahead for the United States, and the world, in the new century.

A WHOLE LOT OF BRAIN POWER

The 1880s and 1890s was the era of the inventor as American hero. Starting with Alexander Graham Bell's unveiling of the telephone in 1876, the last quarter of the nineteenth century saw the introduction of one revolutionary invention after another, everything from aspirin to wireless telegraphy. One inventor after another became the celebrity *du jour*, gracing the covers of magazines while capturing both headlines and the national imagination. It was a time when every day seemed to bring about at least one new innovation, and the world and all its secrets seemed, perhaps for the first time, to be wide open. So did the future.

And one man seemed to be at the center of it all. He was born into a middle-class family in Milan, Ohio, in 1847. As a child, Thomas Edison was labeled "too stupid to learn" by a teacher and asked to leave school. Childhood scarlet fever left him with impaired hearing that would continue to deteriorate for the rest of his life. Still, his ambition and intellectual curiosity became apparent at a very early age. By the time Edison was twelve, he was publishing his own newspaper and selling it on commuter trains.

In 1865, as the Civil War was winding down, Edison

Alexander Graham Bell

enlisted in the Union Army and was stationed in Memphis. He was trained as a telegraph operator, but soon channeled his energies toward inventing. In 1868, at the age of twenty-one, Edison filed his first patent, for a ma-

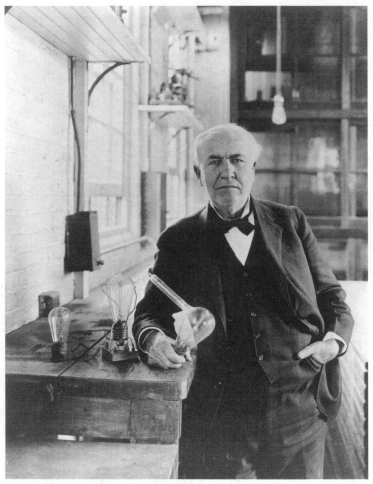

The Wizard of Menlo Park, Thomas Edison

chine that would telegraphically record and report votes. But he had a difficult time selling the machine commercially—mostly, it seems, because many politicians did not want votes to be counted accurately.

Two years later, in 1870, he patented a new stock market ticker, which did become a commercial success. The following year, Edison, now twenty-four years old, moved to Newark, New Jersey, and opened his first machine shop. Six years later, having moved his operations to Menlo Park, he patented what is now regarded as his first great invention—the phonograph—and won overnight international fame.

Not one to rest on his laurels, Edison immediately threw himself into another project: creating a workable electric light. Other electric lights had already been patented, but every one of them suffered a serious flaw that rendered them all but useless; their filaments, which had been constructed of flammable materials and exposed to oxygen, burned out very quickly. Edison labored tirelessly for a year (he once said that genius was "10 percent inspiration and 90 percent perspiration"), testing many different materials, before he concocted a filament, made of carbonized cotton thread, that would not burn out very quickly. Edison successfully tested his new light bulb on October 21, 1879, and introduced it to the public soon thereafter.

Throughout the 1880s, Edison—by now known as the "Wizard of Menlo Park"—continued to work tirelessly in his shop, developing, among other things, a great deal of the technology that made motion pictures possible. He was a pioneer filmmaker and record producer, selling countless projectors, phonographs, lightbulbs, and dictation machines. In his lifetime, he filed a total of 1,097 patents; it is undeniable that the world would look and sound quite different had Thomas Edison never lived. More than just an inventor, he embodied the very spirit of inventing and scientific progress, doing more than anyone else to shape an era that is now recognized as the beginning of the technological age. He died in 1931 at the age of eighty-four.

CHAPTER 2

THE NEW CENTURY

U.S. POPULATION: 75,994,575 (1900) 91,972,266 (1910)

A BIT OF CONTROVERSY

Although a lot of people think the twentieth century began on January 1, 1900, historians see things a little differently. For them, the twentieth century—or, for that matter, any century—isn't merely a matter of mathematics and chronology. Historians see centuries in terms of themes and trends, not years and dates. Some consider the twentieth century to have begun in 1893, when the historian Frederick Jackson Turner declared that the American Frontier was closed; others state that it began in 1898, when the United States defeated Spain in a neat little war and, in the process, became a colonial power for the first time. Some even say the twentieth century began all the way back in April 1865, when Lee surrendered to Grant to end what many consider to be the first truly "modern" war.

But it's interesting to consider the possibility that, academically and historically speaking, the twentieth century in America actually began, to be specific, September 6, 1901. To be even more specific, in Buffalo, New York.

YES, *BUFFALO*, OF ALL PLACES

On September 6, 1901, President William McKinley was in Buffalo to attend the Pan-American Exposition. Mc-Kinley, fifty-eight years old, was just six months into his second term as president; the highlights of his first term were a continuation of his predecessors' friendly policies toward industry and big business, and, of course, the Spanish-American War. McKinley himself was a short, gentle man, a veteran of the Civil War (he entered the Union Army as a private and rose to the rank of major by war's end), former congressman, and governor of Ohio. He was extremely devoted to his invalid wife, and always wore a spotless white vest and a red carnation in his lapel. In other words, he was probably a nicer person than the average late-nineteenth-century president, but otherwise fairly undistinguished.

Leon Czolgosz, though, saw President McKinley as the incarnation of evil. Czolgosz (pronounced CHOL-gotz),

THE FOULEST CRIME OF THE NEW CENTURY.

AN ANARCHIST'S ATTEMPT, AT THE BUFFALO EXPOSITION, TO MURDER THE MOST POPULAR OF ALL AMERICAN PRESIDENTS—DRAWN BY
T. DART WALKER, OUR SPECIAL ARTIST AT THE PAN-AMERICAN EXPOSITION.

The Foulest Crime of the New Century

the twenty-eight-year-old son of Polish immigrants, grew
up in Detroit and Cleveland, and had worked at a series
of factory jobs for the first two decades of his life. In
1893, when workers at his factory organized a strike,
Czolgosz became involved in labor and radical causes.
He flirted with socialism and anarchism, disavowed the
Catholic Church, and joined a series of left-wing organi-

zations. He met some of the leading revolutionaries of the day (including the famous, fiery anarchist orator and organizer Emma Goldman), though they would all, eventually, deny knowing Czolgosz.

Somewhere along the line, Czolgosz decided that President McKinley was a dangerous enemy of working people and the poor. "McKinley was going around the country shouting about prosperity when there was no prosperity for the poor man," he would later write. "One man shouldn't have so much service and another man should have none."

On the afternoon of September 6, 1901, Czolgosz, too, went to the Pan-American Exposition. His express purpose was seeing the president up close. He brought with him a .32-caliber pistol, hidden in his right hand, wrapped in a large handkerchief. A Secret Service agent, spotting Czolgosz's hand, suggested he go to the first-aid station. Czolgosz said he would, after he got to greet the president. McKinley, working his way down a line of visitors, shook Czolgosz's hand and moved on. Czolgosz stepped up behind him and shot the him twice. McKinley fell to the ground. Bodyguards immediately pounced upon Czolgosz and beat him mercilessly. "Be easy with him, boys," McKinley mumbled. Then, "My wife . . . be careful how you tell her. Oh, be careful!" He died eight days later, on September 14.

On September 23, Czolgosz went on trial in Buffalo, charged with first-degree murder. He refused to testify or even talk to his lawyers, and his lawyers, assigned by the court, didn't much seem to care. The whole thing lasted eight and a half hours. To the end, Czolqosz insisted that McKinley had been an enemy of working people and that he had no regrets. On October 29, he was electrocuted.

"THE CRIME OF THE CENTURY"

Stanford White was a true man of his times. The country's most famous turn-of-the-century architect, he designed some of the grandest homes ever seen, and he lived as well as most of his clients. But White's masterpiece was not a private house; it was the original Madison Square Garden, *the* Gilded Age showplace. Its tower was topped by a gold-plated statue of Diana, modeled on one of his mistresses, the stunning Evelyn Nesbit. White and Nesbit had first become involved when she was only sixteen; but White was married, and he refused to leave his wife for Nesbit, who eventually married a Pittsburgh Coke heir named Harry K. Thaw. Thaw was an imbalanced man, obsessed with White and blinded with jealousy and the knowledge that White and his wife had been intimate. On June 25, 1906, Thaw and Nesbit were attending a show at the Garden when they spotted White in the audience. Thaw walked up to White and calmly shot him twice in the head. Nesbit is said to have reacted: "My, Harry! You are in a fix!"

From the moment the smoke cleared, the press became obsessed with the crime, the upcoming trial, and the woman at the center of it all. Every day, newspapers ran her picture and some frivolous story; many had taken to calling it "the crime of the century," obviously unconcerned that the century was still only six years old. Nesbit was expected to testify for the prosecution, but she secretly struck a deal with the defendant and his family. Instead, she testified that White had cruelly beat her, and that her husband, learning of this, had become temporarily insane, shooting White to avenge her honor. The first trial ended in a hung jury; the second ended with Thaw being found not guilty by reason of insanity and sent to an asylum for just a few years. Nesbit, though, never received the large settlement Thaw promised her. He divorced her from the asylum, and she died a half century later, broke and forgotten.

There were two major results of McKinley's assassination. One was that the government, already distrustful of leftists, cracked down on them with a vengeance, arresting hundreds, deporting scores, and keeping untold numbers from ever entering the country at all.

The other major result was that the country was now in the hands of its youngest president ever—McKinley's forty-two-year-old vice president, Theodore Roosevelt.

BULLY FOR THE LITTLE MAN

Theodore Roosevelt has become such a monumental—even legendary—figure in the American imagination that the truth about him is often surprising. The image of TR that most often comes to mind is of a robust, energetic man who was always on the go, was fond of saying "Bully!" to express enthusiasm, and who, when he wasn't running the country, was off hunting big game out West or in the wilds of Africa. In other words, Teddy (as he did *not* like to be called) was a real man's man. And it is true that TR did have what seemed like boundless energy, that he did enjoy hunting and sports, that he did lead a charge up San Juan Hill. It's also true that he was a skinny, asthmatic child, that he had an unusually high-pitched and nasal voice, that he was occasionally prone to depression, and that he was virtually blind without his eyeglasses. Nevertheless, he managed to overcome these setbacks, and more, by sheer force of his personality. He was the consummate politician, and he loved to be the center of attention. "Theodore likes to be the bride at every wedding," a relative once noted, "and the corpse at every funeral."

He was born in New York City in 1858, into a privileged and old Dutch family; his grandfather had been one of the richest men in the city. He idolized his father, Theodore Roosevelt Sr., who instilled in his son an obligation to use his wealth and position to help the less fortunate. As a child, Theodore Jr. was so sickly that he could not attend school, and he was educated entirely by private tutors until he went off to Harvard at the age of eighteen. To overcompensate for his slight build and humorous-sounding voice, he took up boxing, and almost became school champion. As a senior, he began writing his first book, *The Naval War of 1812*, which would be published when he was only twenty-three. That same year, he was elected to the New York State Assembly. And he had already attended Columbia Law School and managed to woo and marry a Boston beauty, Alice Hathaway Lee. The world, it would seem, was his for the asking.

But Roosevelt's life had a tragic vein. When he was just nineteen, his father died; TR was so grief-stricken that he dropped out of Harvard for a while. Then, on February 14, 1884, Alice died, just a day after giving birth to their first child. And in one of those awful coincidences, his mother died on the very same day. It was too much for Roosevelt; he sank into a depression, left the State Assembly, left his infant daughter (Alice, named for her late mother) with an aunt, and headed for the family ranch in the Dakotas, hoping the rigorous lifestyle and solitude would lift his spirits.

It did. Two years later, he returned to New York, ran unsuccessfully for mayor, and married Edith Carow, an old family friend. In 1889, he began a six-year stint as head of the U.S. Civil Service Commission, after which he served two years as president of the New York City Police Commission. In both positions, he made a name for himself as a tireless crusader against corruption. In 1897, President McKinley appointed him Assistant Secretary of the U.S. Navy, a position from which he did all he could to encourage the nation to declare war on Spain. When the war finally came, he raised a regiment of cavalry (known as the Rough Riders), led them in a famous charge up San Juan Hill in Cuba, returned a hero, and promptly got himself elected governor of New York.

As governor, Roosevelt once again attacked corruption and political machinery, while agitating to improve the lot of the poor and disenfranchised. The local Republican Party (of which TR was a member), anxious to get rid of him and return everything to normal, schemed to get him nominated for vice president in 1900. When their scheme worked, though, not everyone was happy about the result. "Don't you realize," lamented the Republican National Committee chairman and top McKinley patron Mark Hanna, "there's only one life between that madman and the presidency?"

On September 14, 1901, that one life slipped away. "Now look!" Hanna cried. "That damned cowboy is President of the United States!"

Nevertheless, the country was wild about Theodore Roosevelt. After all, they had never seen anything like him. He was a generation younger than most presidents, for one thing, and a thoroughly modern man. He was the first president to ride in an automobile, on an airplane, and in a submarine; the first to leave the United States during his term of office; the first to publish a book while in office; the first to appoint a Jew to his cabinet, and to invite an African-American to the White House; and the first (and

President Theodore Roosevelt

only) president to win a Nobel Peace Prize, for heading
the negotiations that ended the Russo-Japanese War in
1905. More than that, though, he was the first president
in memory to adopt the pretense of putting the interests
of the "little man" over those of big business. Whether or
not he really was a "man of the people" is open to debate,
but it is undeniable that Roosevelt brought his now famous
(or infamous) energy and zeal for reform to the White
House, and that *was* something quite new.

BUSTING THOSE TRUSTS
(AND VICE VERSA)

In the first decade of the twentieth century, it was a
revolutionary idea: that big business existed to serve the
national interest, and not vice versa. (Come to think of

GUESS WHO'S COMING TO DINNER: THE ORIGINAL VERSION

On October 16, 1901, just a month after he became president, Theodore Roosevelt welcomed a most unusual dinner guest to the White House: Booker Taliaferro Washington.

Booker T. Washington was born a slave in Virginia in 1856. In 1881, he founded the Tuskegee Institute in Tuskegee, Alabama, the first African-American teachers' college in the country. By the turn of the century, he had become the most prominent African-American in the country, and a founder of what would eventually become the Civil Rights Movement. By modern standards, he was a gradualist, advocating a policy of nonconfrontation and general accommodation toward whites; he believed that American blacks could never achieve equality with whites without first winning whites' affection and respect, a process, he said, that could not be forced. "In all things that are purely social, we can be as separate as the fingers," he advised, "yet one as the hand in all things essential to mutual progress." In other words, Washington believed that it didn't matter if blacks couldn't eat in the same restaurants, live in the same neighborhoods, or travel in

The First American Role Model in the 20th Century

GUESS WHO'S COMING TO DINNER: THE ORIGINAL VERSION (*continued*)

the same train cars as whites, so long as they could get and keep good jobs. It was an approach that appealed to many whites, particularly in the northeast.

Down south, though—and, truth be told, in much of the rest of the country—whites could not get past the color of Washington's skin; to them, he was a black man like any other, and they were shocked and outraged that the president (whose mother had been born in the South) would have the gall and poor taste to actually dine with such a being in the White House. Southern congressmen, senators, and newspaper editors heaped relentless verbal abuse upon Roosevelt, calling him a traitor to his class, his race, and even to the United States; a wave of violence against blacks swept across the South. Roosevelt, chastened, said nothing, and hoped the incident would just fade away. He never invited another African-American to the White House, and it would be decades before any U.S. president did.

it, it's a fairly revolutionary idea today.) It was an idea that Theodore Roosevelt advocated. And it would be put to a test less than a year after he took over at the White House. When it was over, industry and labor both realized that this president was something new—as new as the century itself.

This new approach to big business started on March 10, 1902, when the president authorized his attorney general, Philander C. Knox, to file suit against the Northern Securities Company, a railroad holding company owned largely by J. P. Morgan and Edward Harriman. Northern Securities was what was known as a "trust," an organization that owned every aspect of a particular industry in a particular region. In this case, Northern Securities owned everything needed to manufacture and operate a railroad, including coal mines, steel mills, and, of course, tracks and depots.

In filing his suit, Knox invoked the Sherman Antitrust Act of 1890, which prohibited "every contract, combination in the form of trust or otherwise, or conspiracy, in restraint of trade or commerce among the several States, or with foreign nations," and charged with a misdemeanor "every person who shall monopolize, or attempt to monopolize . . . any part of the trade or commerce." The Sherman Act never actually explained what constituted a monopoly or trust, and offered only vague notions of how to deal with them; needless to say, it was rarely invoked, and so, when Knox used it against Northern Securities, the business and industrial communities were shocked and outraged. After all, the government's

rule regarding business regulation had always been "laissez-faire," or "let it be," in other words, keep the two as separate as church and state. Nevertheless, Knox stood firm, and Roosevelt backed him up, vowing to take it all the way to the Supreme Court, if necessary. It proved necessary, and on March 14, 1904, the Court, with a one-vote majority, ruled against Northern Securities, a decision that stunned big business, delighted the general public, and opened the door to a full-fledged attack on trusts in the courts and the press.

Roosevelt also broke with his predecessors early in his term by backing labor—to an extent. Once again, railroads were the enemy, but this time, the battlegrounds were not courts but coal mines. On May 12, 1902, just two months after Knox filed his suit against the railroads, John Mitchell, head of the United Mine Workers union, declared that he and the union's 140,000 members would go on strike.

The union sought basic concessions, including wage raises, shorter working hours, more secure employment, and the right of miners to live outside company houses (where the company set the rents) and buy supplies outside of the company stores (often, miners were paid only in exchange, a bizarre arrangement that had men working in the mines in order to buy equipment so they could continue working in the mines). Railroad companies, which owned most of the mines, refused to negotiate or even recognize the union. Their attitude was summed up by George F. Baer, the president of the Reading Coal and Iron Company, who explained: "The rights and interest of the laboring man will be protected and cared for, not by the labor agitators, but by the Christian men to whom God, in His infinite wisdom, has given the control of the property interests of His country, and upon the successful management of which so much depends.'' (Here's an interesting party game: Try to count how many things in this statement are offensive by today's standards.)

Thus the strike settled into a stalemate, which dragged on through the summer and into the fall; the price of coal, the nation's leading source of energy, rose from five dollars to thirty dollars a ton. By October, Roosevelt, who had refused to intervene, summoned both sides to the White House and attempted to mediate the conflict, but the owners walked out before any settlement could be reached. Angry, Roosevelt decided that the strike had become a matter of national interest and security, and that he would just have to have the army assume control of the mines. The owners panicked, and agreed, at last, to submit to arbitration. Ultimately, the miners won most of their concessions.

Theodore Roosevelt was an extremely dynamic president who made the most of his seven and a half years in the White House. He campaigned tirelessly for natural conservation; built up the navy and sent it around the world; created the Panama Canal; assumed responsibility for the "welfare" of every nation and state in the Western Hemisphere (whether they wanted it or not); began regulation of the food and pharmaceutical industries; and generally led the nation headlong into the twentieth century. But many people remember him most as an enemy of big business, and labor's first friend in the White House. And, even though he was often at odds with it, he was, in an important sense, the leader of the era's most notable social movement: Progressivism.

NOT TO BE CONFUSED WITH
ANTI-GRESSIVES

It is a peculiar thing about this country, but from time to
time idealism steps forward from the shadows of popular
thought and takes center stage. At these times, prominent
leaders and humble citizens set aside the mundane concerns of day-to-day living and think about the welfare of
other people, even society as a whole. Now, if you're the
kind of person who can't stand having do-gooders nagging
you to look out for your fellow man, don't panic; it doesn't
happen all that often, at least not on a large scale. On the
other hand, if you're one of those idealists, you can take
comfort in the fact that it seems to happen much more
often in the United States than anywhere else in the world.
Hey, this is the country that gave rise to the American
Revolution, the Abolitionist Movement, and countless little
Utopian colonies. So what happened in this country between the Spanish-American War and World War I
shouldn't come as too much of a surprise.

What happened was, quite simply, one of the greatest
periods of Progressivism in several centuries. Now, this
is not to say that this kind of thing hadn't happened
before. It had, no doubt about it. But no doubt, either,
that this was something remarkable. Reformers coming
out of the woodwork. Ideas floating around that were
way, way ahead of their time (and even ours). Some of
them were even pretty good.

And people actually believed in the power of ideas,
small and big, from lowering the price of a subway token
to dismantling the government of the United States and
replacing it with . . . well, with nothing. There were
anarchists, socialists, and people who thought that only

poetry and prose could save America. There were people agitating to secure permanent equality for African-Americans, to organize every American worker into some labor union or other, to turn public utilities over to the people, to make war forever illegal and unthinkable. A half century before the pill and the sexual revolution, there were people, quite a few of them, loudly advocating birth control and "free love," that is, sex outside of marriage. There were those who called for a radical redistribution of American wealth, demanded that America immediately dispossess the territories it had seized from Spain in 1898, insisted that all monopolies be immediately and irreversibly broken up, pleaded for the demise of age-old, corruption-laden political machines like Tammany Hall. Some people even wanted liquor outlawed.

Progressives won women the right to vote, people the right to elect senators and judges directly, to vote in political primaries and on individual referenda. They fought for, and won, a Federal Reserve system, lower tariffs, more progressive taxes, secret ballots, better housing for the poor and working class, government regulation of food and drugs, home rule for cities, universal public education, the right to strike. They never did manage to lower the price of a subway token, but they certainly tried.

They contributed to newspapers, published magazines and journals, printed up millions of leaflets, and stood, literally, on thousands of soapboxes. They were called "freethinkers," "muckrakers," and "radicals." They were middle-class Protestants who grew up in the enlightened, scientific, relieved America that took shape after the Civil War; and immigrant Catholics and Jews, raised in the most oppressive regimes and squalid slums of Europe, people desperately fighting for their lives. Some died young; some were deported or imprisoned for a

WHO'S
H
O
☞

Call them radicals, muckrakers, freethinkers, or visionaries— They were all important to the Progressive movement in the first two decades of this century:

Emma Goldman (1869–1940): Perhaps the most famous figure in the movement, Goldman seemed to be everywhere: anarchist, labor organizer, feminist, free-love advocate, and dramatist, her oratory was so skillful and impassioned that she was always in demand as a speaker, and she was guaranteed to draw a huge crowd. A resident of the United States since 1885, "Red Emma" was arrested in the antileftist crackdowns of 1919 and deported to Russia. She died in exile.

Max Eastman (1883–1969): Born in upstate New York and educated at Harvard, in 1912 Eastman took over a little magazine named *The Masses* and transformed it into the most prominent and powerful voice of the Progressive movement. Eastman published and promoted some of the leading avant-garde voices of his day. Because of its opposition to the war, *The Masses* was shut down by the government in 1918. For a while in the 1920s he was an avid supporter of the Soviet Union, but Eastman gradually drifted to the right, eventually writing for *Reader's Digest* and *The National Review*.

Florence Kelley (1859–1932): Born into a family of privilege, Kelley, the daughter of a Re-

WHO'S
H
O
☛

(*Continued*)

publican congressman from Philadelphia, graduated from Cornell in 1882 and moved to New York, where she became involved in the Progressive reform movement. She agitated for a minimum wage and women's suffrage, among other causes, lived in a settlement house on the Lower East Side of Manhattan, and in 1898 became head of the National Consumers' League, a post she held until her death thirty-four years later.

Jacob Riis (1849–1914): A native of Denmark, Riis came to America in 1870 and went to work as a police reporter for the *New York Tribune*. His work exposed him to the degradation and danger of New York slums, and in 1890 he became famous with the publication of *How the Other Half Lives*, a description of life in Manhattan's squalid Lower East Side, which was then populated almost entirely by hapless immigrants. Riis became a crusader for the cause of reform, and his photographs of tenement life shocked and angered the nation. One of his biggest supporters was Theodore Roosevelt.

Hutchins Hapgood (1869–1944) and Lincoln Steffens (1866–1936): A pair of journalistic crusaders, Hapgood and Steffens worked together and separately to expose corruption, exploitation, and substandard living conditions.

WHO'S WHO ☛

(Continued)

Hapgood wrote for the *New York Commercial Advertiser*, where Steffens was city editor. Like Riis, Hapgood focused his attention on the Lower East Side of Manhattan; his most famous work was *The Spirit of the Ghetto: Studies of the Jewish Quarter in New York*, published in 1902. Around the same time, Steffens rose to national prominence with his series about political corruption, "The Shame of the Cities," published in *McClure's* magazine. Later, Steffens became even more renowned for his coverage of the Russian Revolution.

Margaret Sanger (1879–1966): Trained as a nurse, Sanger became an early advocate of contraception. With her sister, she opened the first birth control clinic in Brooklyn in 1916. The following year, she was arrested for violating New York's anticontraception laws and sentenced to thirty days in jail, where she gave lectures on birth control to her fellow inmates. Sanger continued to agitate for the cause, eventually becoming a founder of Planned Parenthood.

Upton Sinclair (1878–1968): Perhaps the most famous muckraker of all, in 1906 Sinclair published *The Jungle*, an account of his seven weeks working in the meat-packing plants of Chicago. Sinclair's book exposed such nauseating details about the foul conditions of both the meat

WHO'S
H
O
☞

(Continued)

(often diseased and rat-infested) and the meat-packers' living quarters (also often diseased and rat-infested) that the industry begged the government to regulate it, in the hopes of somehow regaining the public's trust, leading to the formation of national pure food and drug laws. Sinclair, a socialist who was almost elected governor of California in 1934, also crusaded against child labor and was a founder of the American Civil Liberties Union.

Ida Tarbell (1857–1944): One of the first famous female journalists and muckrakers, in 1904 Tarbell published *History of the Standard Oil Company*, which exposed the ruthlessness and excesses of John D. Rockefeller's massive trust and fueled the nascent national fervor for trust-busting. She worked at *McClure's* magazine with Lincoln Steffens, and was an avid proponent of tariff reform, but in 1912 she outraged many progressives by publishing *The Business of Being a Woman*, in which she came out against the feminist and women's suffrage movements.

large chunk of their lives. Some grew more conservative as they grew older, and some stayed active and progressive until they died at a ripe old age. And many were forgotten, along with their ideas, after the era came to a close with the First World War. But a few made it pretty

far, like Robert La Follette, who became governor of
Wisconsin and later a U.S. Senator (where he promoted
a national income tax, popular and direct primary elections, and increased federal regulation of trade and industry), and Eugene V. Debs, who, as a Socialist, ran for
president five times, once winning 6 percent of the vote.
At no other time in American history have men and
women outside the political mainstream enjoyed a
higher profile or level of achievement.

BIG MAN, BIG TUB

In 1908, Theodore Roosevelt decided not to antagonize
his opponents by running for a third term as president.
So he retired at age fifty—sort of. Actually, he hand-
picked a successor, helped get the man elected, and left
for Africa to hunt big game, assuming that everything
would be the same when he returned.

President William Howard Taft

The man Roosevelt picked to succeed him was William Howard Taft, a fifty-one-year-old native of Ohio who claimed that being involved in politics "makes me sick." Nevertheless, Taft had served as superior court judge, solicitor general, circuit court justice, civil governor of the Philippines, and, most recently, secretary of war. Taft didn't much want to be president, but Roosevelt wanted it for him, and TR generally got what he wanted. Taft easily defeated William Jennings Bryan at the polls, and settled, somewhat uneasily, into the White House. It is telling to note that Taft might just be remembered most for his special bathtub. He was the largest man ever to serve as chief executive, less than six feet tall but weighing between 300 and 350 pounds, and, well, he didn't quite fit into the old tub, so he ordered a new one. It was so large that the four workmen who installed it could easily sit in it comfortably, and they did so, posing for a rather famous photograph.

If that famous picture is Taft's most prominent legacy, it's not hard to understand why. He was one sorry politician, plain and simple, and he knew it. He lacked the basic skills of tact and diplomacy, and had this nasty habit of falling asleep during cabinet meetings, White House dinners, public ceremonies, and even funerals. He was helplessly bullied by liberal and conservative alike, and was rarely able to commit to a course of action and see it through. He could not remember another person's name to save his own life—perhaps the most important skill any politician can have. Worst of all, he alienated Roosevelt almost immediately after his election, by failing to express proper gratitude to the man who had all but placed him in the White House and by recklessly abandoning many of Roosevelt's initiatives and reforms, especially those related to natural conservation, an issue very dear to TR's heart. Even though he actually increased antitrust prosecution, Taft quickly lost the confidence and support of most progressives, who saw him as a throwback to the Republican "old guard." Perhaps Taft might have survived such a defection if he had not

FILLING OUT THE CONTINENT

Three more states joined the Union during this period, making the continental United States—forty-eight of them, in all—complete:

Oklahoma, November 16, 1907;
New Mexico, January 6, 1912;
Arizona, February 14, 1912.

lost the support of the nation's most prominent progressive—Theodore Roosevelt.

1912: ONE WILD ELECTION

By 1912, Theodore Roosevelt was fifty-four years old and eager to become un-retired. During his four-year hiatus from politics (if you can call it that; he might not have held public office, but he was never far from the halls of power, and he never failed to render an opinion, whether solicited or not), Roosevelt had continued to evolve in his progressive views, and by now, he was personally committed to what he called a program of "new nationalism," which included expanded government regulation of industry and involvement in issues of social welfare. Like many Americans, he perceived that Taft was growing "soft" on these issues. (Ironically, in the fall of 1911, Taft and Roosevelt split bitterly over the giant trust United States Steel; Taft was zealously attempting to break it up, while Roosevelt had, in his own term of office, allowed and even encouraged it to grow.) In June 1912, at the Republican National Convention in Chicago, Roosevelt attempted to hijack the nomination from Taft; he failed, but he did convince a large cabal of progressive Republicans to follow him instead of Taft and walk out of the convention without voting. In August, Roosevelt supporters formed the Progressive Party, nicknamed the Bull Moose Party, in honor of their candidate, who was fond of boasting that he was "as fit as a bull moose."

For his part, their candidate was only too eager to accept the nomination. "I'm throwing my hat into the

ring," Roosevelt said, using a phrase he actually coined.
He then proceeded to barnstorm across the country,
shaking hands and delivering passionate speeches with
as much vigor as ever. By October 14, when he arrived
in Milwaukee, his campaign had acquired great momentum. But leaving his hotel that day, he was shot in the
chest by a deranged saloon-keeper, John F. Schrank. Fortunately, the bullet was slowed down by Roosevelt's steel
eyeglass case and a folded-up copy of his speech (luckily,
it was a long one), and it didn't go very deep into his
chest. TR insisted on delivering the fifty-minute speech before being taken to the hospital. However, he did miss two
weeks on the election trail, at the most crucial time of the
campaign. Still, on November 5, Roosevelt got 27.5 percent
of the popular vote, and eighty-eight electoral votes. Taft,
the incumbent, got just 23 percent of the vote, and eight
electoral votes. Eugene V. Debs, the Socialist candidate, got
6 million votes, his best showing ever.

Roosevelt's strong showing was enough to deny Taft
re-election; in fact, it was the strongest third-candidate
showing in any presidential election in U.S. history.
Still, it was not enough to win; indeed, the true result
of Roosevelt's campaign was to hand the election to
the third major candidate: the Democrat, Woodrow
Wilson.

A PRESBYTERIAN PROFESSOR PREDESTINED FOR THE WHITE HOUSE

Thomas Woodrow Wilson did not take the traditional
path to the White House. For one thing, he was a son
of the South, the first to become president since before

the Civil War; for another, his background was academic, not political or legal. He was a well-known progressive, a thinker, who was considered, by some, too smart to be elected president. And he was a Democrat, the first to be elected president since 1892, and only the second since the Republican Party had come into existence.

Born in Staunton, Virginia, in 1856, the son of a Presbyterian minister, his earliest memories were of the death and destruction wrought by the Civil War (he would be the last president born in the antebellum United States). After college and law school, he earned a Ph.D. in history from Johns Hopkins and embarked upon a teaching career, eventually landing at Princeton, where he authored several books, stood out as a star of the faculty, and helped found the field of political science. In 1902, he was named president of Princeton, and promptly set out on a program of reforms that rejuvenated the old school and transformed it into a world-class university. Four years later, he ran for governor of New Jersey and won in a landslide. Once again, he embarked upon a program of daring and innovative reform (including workman's compensation and regulation of utilities and railroads) that earned the state, and him, a great deal of national attention. By 1912, he was a contender for the Democratic nomination for president.

Still, winning the nomination was a fight, and it took forty-six ballots for Wilson to overcome his major opponent, perennial Democratic candidate William Jennings Bryan. Nevertheless, Wilson left the convention in Baltimore believing that it could have worked out no other way. "I am a Presbyterian and believe in predestination and election," he announced. "It was Providence that did the work in Baltimore." On November 5, he got 42 percent of the popular vote—far less than half, but more than enough to win in a field of three. He was helped by the infighting in the GOP, and by a bitter strike in the mills of Lawrence, Massachusetts, that won a lot of sympathy for the labor movement across the country; but Wilson, again, credited a higher power with his victory. "God ordained that I should be the next President of the United States," he told the chairman of the Democratic National Committee. "Neither you nor any other mortal could have prevented that!"

It was not the kind of modesty that one finds even in most politicians. But, again, Wilson was no ordinary politician.

NOT YOUR TYPICAL FIRST TERM

Perhaps Woodrow Wilson's greatest lasting achievements during his first term were in the economic realm. One of his first major acts as President was to sign into law the Glass-Owen Currency Act of 1913, creating the Federal Reserve System that continues to regulate banking and currency to this day (the Fed, as it is known, operates a dozen Federal Reserve banks across the country, requires member banks to maintain a certain level of cash reserves to insure solvency, and helps set interest rates on loans). The following year, Congress created the Federal Trade Commission—charged with policing industry and maintaining fair competition—and passed the Clayton Anti-Trust Act, which built on the Sherman Act and increased the government's power to challenge and dissolve monopolies.

There were also, two very unusual occurrences during

Woodrow Wilson with Edith Bolling Galt

Wilson's first term in office. The first was that the president became a widower in 1914 when his wife died. Wilson was so distraught he could not leave his room for two days. The following year, though, Wilson was remarried (even though some advisers suggested that doing so might hurt his chances of re-election) to a prominent Washington widow, Edith Bolling Galt.

The second unusual occurrence in Wilson's first term was that the United States invaded Mexico. Twice.

In 1910, a revolution broke out in Mexico against dictator Porfirio Diaz. While then President Taft actually supported Diaz ("We have $2 billion in American capital invested in Mexico that will be greatly endangered if Diaz were to die"), almost no one else did; he was one ruthless, corrupt, and all-around bad guy. The revolutionaries won anyway, and put their man in power, a humane progressive named Francisco Madero. Unfortunately, the United States, mindful of those $2 billion and wary of change—especially when it was coming from the left—wanted the old Diaz days back, and they helped a Mexican general named Victoriano Huerta mount a coup d'etat. Huerta made Diaz look like, well, a decent, honest guy by comparison.

By 1913, Madero had been assassinated, and Huerta had total control over Mexico. By this time, however, there was a new president in town (Washington town, that is), and Wilson was not Taft; he cared a little more about human rights and things like that. Wilson refused to recognize Huerta's presidency of Mexico, stating that Huerta had not been democratically elected. Huerta replied by arresting some U.S. sailors ashore in Tampico. While Huerta soon released the sailors, the tiff spiraled out of control, and . . . well, you know how these things get. On April 21, 1914, Wilson sent the U.S. Navy to seize the port city of Vera Cruz. (The Germans, you see, who supported Huerta—as did almost all European nations, looking to protect their investments—had been shipping arms to the dictator through the port of Vera Cruz. Complicated, isn't it? Well, diplomacy usually is.) Eventually, several South American nations stepped in and prevented a full-blown war from erupting. Huerta, though, was finished, and ultimately fled the country. U.S. troops would remain in Vera Cruz until Thanksgiving. Wilson recognized Huerta's successor, former rebel leader Venustiano Carranza.

Carranza, though, refused to recognize other rebel leaders, including Francisco "Pancho" Villa. In a strangely misguided effort to draw U.S. troops into Mexico (which Villa had hoped would create strife between the Carranza government and the United States), Villa executed eighteen U. S. mining engineers in Mexico. When that didn't work, he gathered up an army of 1,500 men and, on March 9, 1916, crossed the border and attacked the little town of Columbus, New Mexico, killing seventeen townspeople.

That worked. Wilson dispatched 6,000 U.S. troops into Mexico, under the command of Spanish-American War hero John J. Pershing. They never did catch Villa, and eventually Carranza demanded that all U.S. troops clear out of his country. By that time, though, Wilson had bigger problems.

In 1914, a massive war had broken out in Europe. The United States clearly wanted no part of it, and Wilson capitalized on this sentiment. In the election of 1916, he ran under the slogan "He Kept Us Out of War." It worked. He defeated his popular Republican opponent, former U.S. Supreme Court Chief Justice Charles Evans Hughes, in a narrow victory. How narrow? Well, had two thousand California voters changed their choice to Hughes, Wilson would have lost.

But "He Kept Us Out of War" won the day—November 7, 1916—for Wilson.

Five months later, he led us into war.

A NEW WAY OF GETTING AROUND

With two notable exceptions—that is, the locomotive and the steamship—nineteenth-century transportation options were pretty much the same as they had been for thousands of years: on foot, by horse or horse and carriage, or by wind-powered boat. Traversing great distances took a prohibitive amount of time; to the average nineteenth-century American, the world seemed like a very large place. In the 1800s, a great number of Americans never left the county in which they were born; few had traveled outside their home state, much less around the country or the world. The great exception was the Civil War, which took men and boys from isolated farms and small towns, gathered them together in groups larger than any they had ever seen before, and sent them to fight in places they often had never even heard of, much less seen. By and large, though, those who survived returned to their farm or town and resumed the provincial life as best they could.

The automobile, of course, changed all that dramatically.

No single individual is credited with having invented the automobile; it was most certainly not invented in America but rather in Germany and France. The first successful U.S. automobile manufacturers were two brothers—former bicycle mechanics—from Springfield, Massachusetts. In 1893, Charles and Frank Duryea built the first practical automobile powered by a combustion engine; three years later, after their car won the first American automobile race, they started selling their automobiles. By the turn of the century, there were 30 auto manufacturers in the United States, turning out some 2,500 machines a year; by 1910, there would be 485 such companies.

The first truly successful U.S. car was manufactured by Ransom E. Olds. His "Oldsmobile," with its one-cylinder, three-horsepower engine, closely resembled an old-style horse-buggy, except that it was steered by a sail-boat-style tiller. It was heavy, slow, underpowered, and ugly compared with the graceful, beautiful, sleek, and fast automobiles that were then being made in Europe. But the Oldsmobile was sturdy and reliable, and, with a price sticker of about $650, it was affordable to middle-class America. By 1904, Olds was selling 5,500 of them a year.

But the car that truly revolutionized the auto industry, and the nation, made its debut in 1908. Henry Ford had already had some success with his Model N, a four-cylinder, fifteen-horsepower machine that sold for about $600. By 1907, in fact, he was producing a hundred of them a day, and he could barely keep up with orders. Recognizing the immense demand for a "car for the multitude"—affordable and durable, cheap and easy to

Henry Ford and the "Tin Lizzie," 1908

The Wright Brothers

maintain and repair—Ford introduced his Model T. Nicknamed the "Flivver" and the "Tin Lizzie" (don't ask why), the Model T originally sold for $825, although the price would eventually drop to $290. Over the next two decades, Ford made and sold 15 million of them, making the United States an "auto nation" and himself one of the richest men in that nation. To keep up with demand, he developed an assembly-line system of mass production that is still used in auto manufacturing and in countless other industries.

Meanwhile, in 1903, two other brothers and bicycle mechanics from Dayton, Ohio, Orville and Wilbur Wright, went down to Kitty Hawk, North Carolina, and successfully tested the world's first "aeroplane"—a glider capable of taking off and sailing through the air under its own power. The airplane, of course, would eventually do more than the automobile to shrink the world and even shape it. Throughout the first decade of the twentieth century, hundreds of American "aeronauts" would design and build hundreds of novel and bizarre flying machines, some of which actually flew. By World War I, the airplane would be used to drop bombs and deliver mail. But the airplane would not truly become a popular means of mass transportation until after World War II.

WORLD WAR I

Now, Wait a Minute . . .

When President Woodrow Wilson ran for re-election in 1916, he campaigned on the slogan "He Kept Us Out of War." It worked; he won. That was on November 7.

On April 2, 1917, less than five months later, President Wilson asked Congress to declare war on Germany, insisting that "the world must be made safe for Democracy."

So . . . what happened?

A German Public Relations Disaster

Why exactly were the "Allied Powers" (Great Britain, France, Russia, and an amalgam of their various remote outposts and colonies) and the "Central Powers" (Germany, the Austro-Hungarian Empire, the Ottoman Empire, and their assorted outposts and colonies) so intent on destroying each other that they dove into a war that would last four years and cost some 10 million lives? Entire books have been written to answer that question. In the end it always seems to come down to this: A series of ancient grudges and modern entanglements playing out against a backdrop of crumbling empires, new and expansionist powers, egos, and greed. In short, it was the bloody but inevitable culmination of a thousand years of ruthless, treacherous continental (and later global) power struggles. Confused yet? Hey, I *told* you it was a subject for a book, not a paragraph. Anyway, the important thing to remember is that it was a thoroughly, completely European war, as alien to the American character and history as the metric system. The people who started the whole thing could hardly make sense of it; how on earth could we?

We couldn't. We didn't. And we tried to stay out of it, at least for a while.

When war broke out in Europe in the summer of 1914, Americans were ambivalent. Many favored one side or the other, but few actually wanted to fight. As the war dragged on and casualties soared, this attitude became more and more entrenched. Enter a war in which hundreds of thousands of men were killed over a few hundred yards of worthless battlefield? Not for us, thanks. (Hey, we were cocky, but we weren't crazy.)

From the beginning, though, the Allies—especially Great Britain—were looking across the Atlantic and salivating at the thought of drawing the United States into the war on their side. After all, when it came to the three

Ms of warfare—munitions, manpower, and money—
America was a rich nation, one that would make an in-
valuable ally.

So Britain got to work. The first thing they did was
cut the transatlantic cable that connected Europe and
America. This meant that any news the United States
would get via telegraph about the war—or anything else
that might be happening on the other side of the
ocean—would have to go through England. Then they
made certain that they only passed on the most grisly,
sensational stories about Germany. (It was the British,
after all, who invented the tabloid newspaper.)

Germany, meanwhile, gave the British a lot of material
to work with. Early on, they responded to a devastating
allied blockade by using their new submarines—the now
infamous U-boats—to sink Allied ships on the open seas.
At first, the Germans targeted only warships, taking care
to steer clear of neutral ships, especially U.S. ships. But
on May 7, 1915, Germany sank a huge British luxury
liner, the *Lusitania*. The ship—which was probably carrying munitions to Britain, as well as tourists—went
under in a mere fifteen minutes, with a loss of 1,198
passengers, 114 of them Americans. From that day on,
the United States began moving closer and closer to war
with Germany.

NEXT TIME, USE A *SECURED* LINE

Early in the war, President Wilson had the U. S. Navy
set up facilities for wireless transatlantic communications;
he then allowed diplomats on all sides to use these facilities to send messages, even encoded messages. The Ger-

mans, thinking no one could break their code, started using the facilities to send highly sensitive messages. Not a smart move.

On January 17, 1917, British intelligence intercepted and decoded one such wireless telegram, which was sent from Germany's foreign secretary, Arthur von Zimmerman, to Germany's ambassador in Washington, Count Johann von Bernstorff. The message, in which Germany exhibited a keen understanding of U.S. history, read:

> We intend to begin unrestricted submarine warfare. We shall endeavor to keep the United States neutral. In the event of this not succeeding we make Mexico a proposal of alliance on the

following basis: Make war together,
make peace together, generous financial support, and an understanding on our part that Mexico is to
recover the lost territory in Texas,
New Mexico, and Arizona.

The British held onto the telegram—now known as "the
Zimmerman note"—and waited for a good moment to
break the news to President Wilson. On January 31, Germany informed the United States that it would begin
unrestricted submarine warfare on the high seas. Four
days later, America severed diplomatic relations with
Germany. Over the next two months, German U-boats
sank five U.S. ships.

At last the British had found their moment. They
passed the Zimmerman note on to President Wilson.
The rest, as they say, is . . . well, you know.

OVER *WHERE?*

Congress formally declared war on Germany on April 6,
1917. But America's standing army was rather small, and
the rush of enlistments following President Wilson's call
to arms was not nearly enough. A few hundred thousand
men weren't going to make the world safe for democracy; America needed an army of millions. This, then,
brings us to the draft.

On May 18, 1917, Congress passed the Selective Service
Act, authorizing conscription for only the second time in
U.S. history. (The first time, in 1863, draftees had been
allowed to pay a fee of $300 which enabled them to hire

a "substitute" for the duration of the war; this arrangement had led to the New York Draft Riots and other unfortunate incidents.) The act mandated that all men between the ages of twenty-one and thirty register to be drafted for military service. Later, the age limits were widened to eighteen to forty-five. By the end of 1917, some 180,000 U.S. soldiers would be serving in France; by the end of 1918, that number would grow to 2 million.

The nation's first draft in progress

The war—and especially the draft—were extremely unpopular in some places, particularly cities with large first- and second-generation immigrant populations. Many German-Americans resented the demonization of Germany; many Irish-Americans despised the idea of fighting for Great Britain, while many Jewish-Americans felt the same way about czarist Russia. In New York, Mayor John Purroy Mitchel, who avidly supported U.S. entry to the war, was easily defeated by a more neutral Tammany Hall candidate. (Mitchel, who was then thirty-eight years old, enlisted in the Army Air Corps; he was killed during a training flight when he fell out of his plane, having failed to fasten his seat belt. Let that be a lesson to you.) Many other Americans opposed the war on principle; it was a European conflict, they reasoned, and had nothing to do with us. Americans had no business fighting, and dying, for bloated old empires and bloated old emperors.

Nevertheless, in some circles, war fever ran high. Movie and theater stars were recruited to encourage enlistment and to sell war bonds; songwriters, among the top celebrities of the day, did their part by writing a slew of patriotic songs. The most popular of them, "Over There," was penned by George M. Cohan, one of the musical theater's brightest lights, the man who wrote "Give My Regards to Broadway" and "Yankee Doodle Dandy." The song, which announced that "the Yanks are coming," ended with the promise:

> *We'll be over, we're coming over,*
> *And we won't come back*
> *'til it's over Over There!*

"Over There" quickly became America's Great War anthem, even if most Americans weren't quite sure where exactly "there" was or what was waiting for them once they got there.

WHO'S IN CHARGE HERE, ANYWAY?

They called him "Black Jack," not because he was skilled with a deck of cards, but because he had commanded African-American troops in Cuba during the Spanish-

MORE WORLD WAR I SONG TITLES
Believe it or not, they're all for real:

"Just Like Washington Crossed the Delaware, General Pershing Will Cross the Rhine";

"When I Send You a Picture of Berlin, You'll Know It's Over Over There";

"Keep Your Head Down, Fritzie Boy";

"Lafayette, We Hear You Calling";

"Good-bye, Broadway; Hello, France";

"I Can Always Find a Little Sunshine at the YMCA";

"There's a Service Flag Flying at Our House";

"Khaki Sammy";

"All Aboard for Home Sweet Home";

"The Navy Will Bring Them Back."

American War. In 1916, President Wilson had sent him to Mexico to capture rebel leader and border ruffian Pancho Villa. He never did catch Villa, but the following year, the president came calling again, this time with a better offer: commander in chief of the American Expeditionary Forces (AEF) in France. "Black Jack" General John Joseph Pershing—accepted.

Pershing and the first of the AEF troops arrived in France on June 24, 1917. On July 4, one of his officers, Colonel Charles E. Stanton, stood at the tomb of the Marquis de Lafayette and declared: "Lafayette, we are here." (History does not record if the great French general responded.)

The arrival of General Pershing and the AEF troops in France.

British and French generals were anxious to incorporate this multitude of fresh U.S. soldiers into their battle-weary armies, where some soldiers had been fighting for three long years. Not so fast, Pershing told them. He had been issued strict orders to keep the AEF a "distinct and separate component" of the Allied war effort. In other words, U.S. troops would only be sent into battle under U.S. generals.

PAY UP, SLACKER

War is always an expensive venture, what with the cost of ships and airplanes, guns and artillery, soldiers' salaries and rifles. And those uniforms aren't free, either. So to help pay for making the world safe for democracy, the government issued Liberty Bonds, and undertook the task of selling them to the general public. A favorite venue was the Bond Rally, a cross between a pep rally and a church revival, where movie stars like Douglas Fairbanks and Mary Pickford encouraged the audience to do their patriotic duty by forking over some cash. Songwriters also joined in, like Gus Kahn and Egbert Van Alstyne; their contribution to the war effort was the ditty "What Are You Going to Do to Help the Boys?" which attempted to shame civilians into contributing:

A Bond Rally with Douglas Fairbanks and Mary Pickford

What are you going to do for Uncle Sammy?
What are you going to do to help the boys?
If you need to stay at home while they're fighting o'er the foam,
The least that you can do is buy a Liberty Bond or two.
If you want to be a sympathetic miser,
The kind that only lends a lot of noise,
You're no better than the one who loves the Kaiser—
So, what are you going to do to help the boys?

AND WHILE YOU'RE AT IT, TIGHTEN THAT BELT

On April 4, 1917, two days after he asked Congress to declare war on Germany, President Wilson created the Committee on Public Information, or CPI. Its goal was to educate U.S. citizens about the war in Europe and why it was a good thing we were getting involved in it. In other words, the CPI was a propaganda machine—but it was *our* propaganda machine.

The CPI trained tens of thousands of men to deliver rousing patriotic speeches, then dispatched them to schools, theaters, churches, movie houses, and town halls around the country. It organized massive rallies in major cities, and produced stirring movies like *The Kaiser: The Beast of Berlin*, which may still be on the shelves of your local video store. Most important, the CPI distributed 75 million pamphlets as part of the War Information Series. Titles included "The War Message and the Facts Behind It," "A War of Self-Defense," "The Government of Germany," and "American Loyalty by Citizens of German Descent." Seventy-five million pamphlets, at a time when the country's population was around a 100 million.

The CPI was one of the most prominent government agencies during the war; others included the War Labor Board and the War Industries Board (the latter chaired by millionaire financier Bernard Baruch, who would later accompany President Wilson to Versailles and would remain actively involved in Democratic politics for the next half-century). The agencies were responsible for coordinating the industrial contribution to the war effort (including armaments, uniforms, vehicles, and supplies), keeping the workforce active and happy, and heading off strikes, which would have disrupted production at a time when the country could ill afford it.

And then there was another agency, rather obscure in the war's early days, that would ultimately help catapult its director into the highest office in the nation.

WHAT ABOUT FRIDAYS?

It may seem like a bit of a resume-builder today, but back in 1917 a little-known mining engineer named Herbert Hoover was proud to accept President Wilson's appointment as United States Food Administrator. Actually, it wasn't just a hollow title; the Food Administration quickly assumed control over food and fuel, and fixed the price of wheat, buying huge amounts of it and storing or selling it as the need arose.

Hoover quickly coined the slogan "Food Can Win the War," and set out to encourage farmers to do their part to make the world . . . well, you know. He also prevailed upon average citizens to do their part by observing "Meatless Mondays" and "Wheatless Wednesdays." These programs, and general food rationing, were en-

tirely voluntary, but Hoover's moral authority, coupled
with the patriotic fervor that swept the country in 1917
and 1918, insured near-universal compliance. Most people understood that it was important, as Hoover explained, that "the boys" be fed well and regularly; but
the Food Administrator also shipped tons of desperately
needed edibles to Europe, where the war (and especially
hostile naval blockades) had created near-famine conditions throughout the continent. After the war, Hoover
would head the American Relief Administration, taking
on the even tougher task of keeping millions of Europeans from starving to death during the often chaotic
"peace" of 1919; he would be one of the most popular
men in America, hailed as the savior of Europe.

So Herbert Hoover and the United States Food Administration were among the greatest success stories of the war,
doing well, as they say, by doing good. But on other sectors
of the Home Front, the war was not so benign.

UH, IT'S ACTUALLY A *DUTCH* NAME

When the United States declared war in 1917, it was not
a good time to be a German-American. Germans had been
settling in America since colonial times; thousands had
fought for the Continental Army in the Revolution. But
now Germany was the enemy, and Americans with German
names—many of whom were now soldiers in the American
Expeditionary Force—were regarded with suspicion, even
contempt. Many were forced to Anglicize their surnames
to avoid losing their jobs and being harassed or attacked.
Towns and cities shut down German-language newspa-

pers, outlawed the singing of German songs or even speaking German. Schools banished German from their curriculum; German-Americans were attacked by mobs, their homes and businesses burned and destroyed. They were commonly called *Kraut, Hun, Heinie,* and *Fritz,* not just on the streets but in political speeches, patriotic plays, and popular songs. Even sauerkraut wasn't spared; it was renamed "liberty cabbage" for the duration of the war.

Things weren't any better for other, non–German-Americans who dared object to U.S. participation in the war. Nicholas Murray Butler, the president of Columbia University, declared that any professor who opposed the war would be dismissed. Other colleges and businesses did the same. Congress passed the Espionage and Sedition Acts, which allowed for the imprisonment of war protesters and pacifists; the Supreme Court eventually upheld the laws. Conscientious objectors were sent to federal penitentiaries for refusing to serve in the army, often for religious reasons. Socialist leader Eugene V. Debs was sentenced to ten years at the Atlanta Federal Penitentiary for vocally opposing the war. In 1920, while still in prison (he was released after three years), Debs ran for president. He received nearly a million votes.

MEANWHILE, BACK AT THE FRONT . . .

For more than a year after the United States entered the war, U.S. troops saw relatively little action and managed to avoid serious casualties. That changed in the spring of 1918, when the German Army launched a massive offensive on the western front.

WHO'S
H
O
☞

Douglas MacArthur (1880–1964): A graduate of West Point, class of 1903, MacArthur was already a combat veteran when the United States entered the Great War, having seen action in Mexico. He was commissioned a brigade commander and placed in charge of the celebrated Forty-second Division of the army, known as the "Rainbow Division" because it contained recruits from all forty-eight States.

Harry S Truman (1884–1972): By 1917, Truman was thirty-three years old and had already failed in several business ventures. He enlisted in the army and was sent to France as a captain of artillery. When the war was over, he returned home, joined the Reserve Officer Corps, and embarked upon a career in politics.

Irving Berlin (1888–1989): Born Israel Baline in Russia, Berlin had immigrated to the United States as a child. By the time he was drafted in 1917, he had already made a name for himself as a songwriter for vaudeville and Broadway musical theater. Stationed at Fort Upton in Yaphank, New York, Berlin wrote "Yip-Yip-Yaphank," a musical revue that featured a cast of GIs and opened in New York in 1918. A highlight was the song "Oh, How I Hate to Get Up in the Morning," which quickly became an unofficial (and somewhat subversive) army anthem.

WHO'S H O ☛

(*Continued*)

Eddie Rickenbacker (1890–1973): A well-known racecar driver, Rickenbacker originally went to France as General Pershing's driver. After learning to fly in his spare time, he was assigned to the U.S. Army's 94th Aero Squadron in March 1918. He eventually shot down at least twenty-six German aircraft, making him America's top air ace and earning him the Congressional Medal of Honor. After the war he went into business, ultimately becoming the chairman of Eastern Airlines.

Alvin C. York (1888–1964): A farmer from the mountains of eastern Tennessee, York opposed the war on religious grounds but was denied an exemption from the draft as a conscientious objector. Rather than serve jail time, York went to war; on October 8, 1918, at the height of the Argonne offensive, he single-handedly killed 25 Germans and captured 132 German prisoners and 35 machine guns. He returned home a hero; the city of New York threw him a ticker-tape parade and named York Avenue (formerly Avenue A) for him. In 1941, he was portrayed by Gary Cooper in the film *Sergeant York*.

British and French leaders again implored General Pershing to allow his U.S. troops to be incorporated into larger Allied units. This time, Pershing relented—slightly. U.S. troops would be allowed to fight as a part of larger

Allied units, when necessary. But the general saw to it that
U.S. divisions were not split up and re-assigned, and he
always kept a close eye on how his troops were being used.

Throughout the spring of 1918, U.S. soldiers fought in
some major battles, including Chantigny and Chateau-
Thierry and Belleau Wood, where they sustained heavy
losses. In August, Pershing formed the First U.S. Army,
which was quickly assigned to a crucial sector of the front.
In early September, U.S. troops caught the Germans off
guard at Saint-Mihiel; later that month, they launched what
would be the final great offensive of the war, in the Argonne forest. There, the Americans met fierce resistance
from German troops, who were far more experienced and
who inflicted severe casualties on the "doughboys" (so-
called because of their fondness for that old American staple, the doughnut); eventually, General Pershing sent
more than a million of his troops into the forest, and the
manpower alone overwhelmed the German Army. With a
million more fresh U.S. troops waiting to enter the fight,
Germany came to the conclusion that victory on the battlefield was no longer a possibility. In the second week of
November 1918, Germany sued for peace.

ELEVEN: THE MAGIC NUMBER

The Great War was a great big mess. No way was it going
to be cleaned up overnight. And, with thousands of soldiers dying every day, the first priority was to stop the
fighting. The peace itself could be ironed out later.

So, what Germany requested—and got—in November
1918 was not a formal peace treaty but an armistice, literally a truce, or a temporary suspension of hostilities. In

11:00 AM on November 11, 1918. Two men, one pen, and war ends.

exchange, Germany and the Central Powers would "surrender" to the Allies and submit to Allied terms of peace.

And so, the two sides met at the headquarters of France's military leader, Marshal Ferdinand Foch (the HQ was located in a railroad car in the Forest of Compeigne, outside of Paris), and agreed to stop shooting at each other. The agreement took effect the moment it was signed—at 11:00 A.M. on November 11, 1918, the eleventh hour of the eleventh day of the eleventh month.

At precisely that moment, as a messenger arrived bringing news of the Armistice, Private Henry Gunther of Baltimore, Maryland, a soldier in Company A of the 313th Infantry of the 79th Division of the United States Army, was shot while charging a German machine-gun nest near Metz, France. Private Gunther thus earned the dubious honor of being the last soldier killed in World War I.

The first U.S. battle deaths—three of them—occurred on November 4, 1917. By 11:00 A.M. on November 11, 1918, bullets, bayonets, barbed wire, artillery shells, land mines, torpedoes, poison gas, and disease claimed the lives of 115,660 U.S. soldiers.

ADDING INFLUENZA TO INJURY

In the fall of 1918, just when Americans thought the killing was coming to an end, they got hit with a dose of the worst pandemic the world had seen since the bubonic plague: Spanish influenza. Before you go off and start another Spanish-American War, you should know that the epidemic actually started in China; the Spanish, in fact, were hit very hard: nearly 80 percent of that country was infected.

The disease probably came to this country through two U.S. sailors, who reported sick in Boston on August 27. Within a month, the disease had spread across the coast. Ultimately, a quarter of the United States would catch the disease; in cities and towns across the country, people set up emergency tent hospitals to accommodate the overflow. Schools and other public facilities were closed. People were encouraged to wear face masks to avoid catching the disease; public events, like bond rallies and parades, were canceled for fear of spreading the disease.

And coffins were scarce. The disease claimed 500,000 American lives that fall. Sadly, it seems that Americans weren't even the worst hit. Worldwide, Spanish influenza killed 21.6 million people—more than one percent of the world population, more than twice the number killed in four years of bloody warfare.

FOURTEEN IS *NOT* THE MAGIC NUMBER

President Wilson hadn't had anything to do with planning the war, but four years later, he wanted to plan the peace. In January 1918, Wilson devised a program for peace in the postwar world; it was built around fourteen idealistic goals, and soon became widely known as Wilson's Fourteen Points. On December 4, 1918, Wilson set sail for Europe as the head of the American Delegation to the Peace Conference in Paris. Wilson arrived in Paris full of optimism, convinced that the Allies would see the wisdom of his high-minded and compassionate plan.

No such luck. The European Allies, who had lost millions of men and billions of dollars over the previous four years, were more interested in revenge than in peace. They demanded that Germany accept full blame for the war, cede territories and overseas colonies to the Allies, and pay $15 billion in reparations. Then they bickered and haggled over every one of Wilson's Fourteen Points except the last, which called for the formation of a League of Nations to arbitrate international disputes.

Dejected, Wilson sailed home, only to face a new batch of troubles. It seems that the Republican congress was a tad angry at Wilson for failing to invite a single Republican to join the peace delegation, not to mention the fact that they viewed Wilson's Fourteen Points and the Peace Treaty—named for Versailles, where it was signed—as dangerous international entanglements. Wilson decided to take his case directly to the people, and set off on a whirlwind cross-country tour to promote American participation in the League of Nations. But his health was already frail, and the tour proved to be too much of a

PRESIDENT WILSON'S FOURTEEN POINTS

1. Open covenants of peace, openly arrived at.

2. Freedom of the seas in war and peace.

3. The removal of all economic barriers.

4. Guaranteed reduction of armaments.

5. Impartial adjustment of all colonial claims, with the interests of the subject populations being equal with the claims of governments.

6. Evacuation of all Russian territory.

7. Restoration of Belgian sovereignty.

8. Occupied French territory to be restored, and Alsace-Lorraine to be returned to France.

9. Readjustment of Italian frontiers "along clearly recognized lines of nationality."

10. The people of Austro-Hungary to be given the opportunity for autonomous development.

11. Evacuation by occupying forces of Serbia, Romania, and Montenegro. Relations of Balkan states to be settled along lines of allegiance and nationality. Serbia to be given free access to the sea.

12. Non-Turkish peoples within the Ottoman Empire to be given the opportunity for autonomous development. The Dardanelles to be kept free and open for all shipping.

13. Creation of an independent Poland, with access to the sea.

14. Formation of a League of Nations, with the goal of "affording mutual guarantees of political independence and territorial integrity to great and small states."

strain. On September 25, 1919, he suffered a stroke in Colorado. Two months later, the Senate refused to ratify the Treaty of Versailles and officially rejected membership in the League of Nations.

The president never really recovered from his stroke. For the rest of his term, his duties were largely handled by the first lady, Edith Bolling Galt Wilson. Woodrow Wilson died on February 3, 1924—perhaps the last casualty of World War I.

CHAPTER 4

THE TWENTIES
U.S. POPULATION:
105, 710, 620 (1920)

HMMM . . .

The Roaring Twenties, as they are now remembered, didn't get off to a roaring start. On January 1, 1920, United States Attorney General A. Mitchell Palmer launched simultaneous nighttime raids in thirty-three U.S. cities, arresting more than 4,000 people for being Communist or Russian or "subversive" or "suspicious" or merely in the wrong place at the wrong time. Many who had done nothing at all were nevertheless jailed for days, even weeks.

Two weeks later, on January 16, the Eighteenth Amendment to the Constitution took effect, making it illegal to manufacture, sell, or transport alcoholic beverages anywhere in the United States of America.

It was all uphill from there.

1919: A BAD TIME TO BE A PROGRESSIVE ALCOHOLIC . . .

The temperance movement had been slowly building in this country since the Civil War. By 1916, twenty-one of forty-eight states had gone "dry"; Congress itself was dominated by dry congressmen, who outnumbered "wets" two to one.

Then the war came along and turned the heat up a few notches. The trauma of the war was a catalyst for several social movements, most of them conservative reactions to the battlefield casualties that many believed were a direct result of Progressivism. Progressives were all for meddling in other people's problems and shaking things up, and it was those misguided ideals that had dragged us into a bloody mess that was really none of our business. Or so the reasoning went.

A related line of reasoning, one that gained a certain measure of popularity during and after Lenin's Russian Revolution of November 1917, was that alcoholism was a tool of Bolshevism, used by the latter to weaken the working masses and render them susceptible to the global spread of Communism. This argument might not have convinced a majority of Americans, but it was enough, at that time, to drive the last nail into liquor's coffin. In December 1917, Congress submitted the Eighteenth Amendment to the states for consideration; it was ratified in 1919.

By that time, the campaign against Progressivism had taken on a life of its own. The United States was in the throes of its very first "red scare" following the Russian Revolution of November 1917. The United States had intervened in the ensuing civil war, sending troops to help the "whites" fight the "reds" on Russian soil, but to no avail. Now, a war-weary nation was concerned—to say the least—that the Bolsheviks in Russia would try to spread Communism all over the world. Many believed that Soviet agents were already at work in the United States, doing their best to foment revolution by organizing labor unions, agitating for racial equality and women's rights, and bad-mouthing big business. Those pesky progressives again! (Progressives were not necessarily communists, and vice versa—in fact, in some cases they were bitter enemies—but many on the political right viewed Communism as nothing more than the Progressive movement *du jour.*)

Attorney General Palmer decided to nip the revolution in the bud. Using the Espionage and Sedition Acts left over from the war, Palmer arrested 249 foreign-born radicals, socialists, and anarchists, most of whom had done nothing more than voice opposition to the U.S. form of government. In the final days of 1919, he deported them to Europe. None were ever allowed to re-enter the United States.

. . . BUT A GOOD TIME TO BE A POLITICALLY MINDED WOMAN

The women's suffrage movement, which could trace its roots back to the Seneca Falls Convention (led by Susan B. Anthony) of 1848, had made very slow progress until the second decade of the twentieth century, when those pesky progressives finally managed to adopt a cause that everyone could agree upon: giving women the vote. Certainly, it seemed less dangerous to conservatives than some of their other ideas, like child labor laws and the eight-hour workday.

Early Suffragette

By 1916, both the Democratic and Republican parties officially supported women's suffrage. Things got sidetracked a bit by the war, but in 1919, Congress approved the Nineteenth Amendment, giving women the vote in every state and territory. The next year, the states ratified it, just in time for the 1920 presidential election.

Which, as it turned out, might not have been such a good thing. The wry and reactionary among us still point to the 1920 election and note that the first time women had the vote, they managed to elect a president whose greatest asset was that he *looked* like a president.

TRY RETURNING TO THE DICTIONARY, WHILE YOU'RE AT IT

Let's face it: Warren Gamaliel Harding did look like a president, certainly more so than, say, Millard Fillmore or Grover Cleveland. He was tall, with steel-gray hair and a sharp jawline. The problem was, he didn't *think* like a president; to hear some tell it, he didn't even think much at all.

Harding was born near Blooming Grove, Ohio, in 1865. After college, he took over a daily newspaper in Marion, Ohio, married a wealthy woman—Florence Wolfe, who was five years his senior—and gradually eased into state Republican politics. After a couple of terms in the state senate, and another as lieutenant governor, he ran for governor in 1910.

He lost. But in 1914, he ran in Ohio's first popular election for the U.S. Senate, and won. Again, it was those looks of his that sealed the deal. As a senator, Harding was known mostly for his charm and his ability to make peace and get along with just about everyone. He didn't seem to *do* very much—he never sponsored a single successful bill—but his colleagues liked him pretty well, anyway.

President Warren Gamaliel Harding

In 1920, as the Republican National Convention deadlocked over whom to nominate for president, Harding's name was thrown into the ring on the tenth ballot. He won the nomination and hit the road, giving long-winded speeches in which he tortured the English language. Harding, the former newspaper editor, thought he knew the language pretty well; others disagreed, and labeled the candidate's brand of speech "Gamalielese."

The most famous example occurred during a speech in Boston when Harding asserted that what America really needed was "not nostrums but normalcy." He had meant to say "normality," but had flubbed the line. No matter. The GOP seized the expression "a Return to Normalcy" as a campaign slogan.

It worked. The country, it turned out, wanted nothing more than "a return to normalcy" (even if it wasn't in the dictionary) after the upheaval of the First World War. Harding easily defeated his Democratic opponent, James M. Cox, in November.

The man did *look* like a president.

PRESIDENT HARDING: HE . . . UH . . . WASN'T A GIRL

It's a difficult thing to find anyone who has a good thing to say about Warren Gamaliel Harding. Journalist H. L. Mencken was driven to distraction by Harding's mangling of the English language. "It reminds me of . . . dogs barking idiotically through endless nights," he said. "It is so bad that a sort of grandeur creeps into it."

Alice Roosevelt Longworth, the late president's daughter, was a little more generous. "Harding was not a bad man," she said. "He was just a slob."

Historians almost uniformly rate him the worst president in U.S. history. Even his father had something to say. "If you were a girl, Warren," he told his son, "you'd be in the family way all the time. You can't say no."

THIS YOU CALL NORMALCY?

The country Harding took over on March 4, 1921, was dry. Not dry like the wit of his vice president, Calvin Coolidge (we'll get to him later), but dry in terms of alcohol consumption. But even that's not very accurate. The truth is, in many places, Prohibition did not do very much to curb the consumption of alcohol; in some, it actually increased it.

In the parts of the country—most of them rural—that had voluntarily gone "dry" prior to Prohibition, the new rule caused little stir. In the big cities, where the steady stream of alcohol was abruptly dammed up at 12:01 A.M. on January 16, 1920, things were a bit different. Yes, alcohol ceased to be sold and consumed openly in bars, clubs, and restaurants. But it hardly disappeared; it merely went underground.

You see, a lot more thought had gone into enacting Prohibition than had gone into actually enforcing it. Responsibility for enforcement was entrusted with the Treasury Department—go figure—which, needless to say, didn't have too much experience with this sort of thing. Problems immediately arose.

The United States, of course, has many thousands of

Old Gin Still with Attendant

miles of border with Canada and Mexico, and thousands more of coastline along various oceans, gulfs, and bays. There are a lot of places for a little old smuggler to sneak a boat or two of contraband past the authorities, especially undermanned, inexperienced authorities. The smugglers might have been undermanned and inexperienced, too, but they stood to make a whole lot of money in the process, and they got experience in a hurry.

Naturally, this raised the price of the product. You would think that this development might price poor and middle-class consumers out of the market for the good stuff. You would be right. But the United States also has a long and revered history of "bootlegging"—cooking up the stuff yourself in a home-made still. (The term "bootlegging" comes from the practice of sneaking a flask of this illegal hooch around in the leg of a boot.) Before Prohibition, the stereotypical bootlegger could be found in some remote mountaintop shack down South. During Prohibition, he could be found just about everywhere. And for those who just had to have a drink but couldn't afford steep "import duties," the bootlegger became indispensable.

Ironically, making alcohol illegal only raised its allure and cachet in many circles, and in cities and towns across the country, "speakeasies," or underground nightclubs, flourished, creating a whole new class of millionaires. In addition to speakeasy owners, smugglers got rich. So did gangsters, who had formerly been limited to the small-time exploits of money lending, running numbers, and protection rackets. Prohibition opened up a whole new world—sneaking booze across borders, running it through Coast Guard blockades, trucking it around the country. As the risks increased, so did profits—and violence between competitors. People soon came to realize that while Prohibition may have put a dent in public drunkenness, it opened the door wide to entirely new classes of lawlessness, and they started to question the wisdom of the Eighteenth Amendment.

FLAPPERS AND FADS

A popular 1920s archetype was the flapper, a stick-thin party girl with bobbed hair, a long string of pearls, short skirt, fashionable hat, and an unquenchable thirst for fun. And there was always plenty of fun to be had. The flapper was, herself, the personification of one of the decade's greatest expressions of fun: the fad.

The twenties was a decade of fads. There were dance crazes, like the Charleston and the fox-trot; fashion trends, like the knee-length string of pearls and the raccoon coat; and absurd tests of endurance, like flagpole sitting, goldfish swallowing, and seventy-two-hour dance marathons. Of all the twenties fads, though, the one that most captured the national imagination was barnstorming, increasingly outrageous stunts performed by daredevil pilots. In addition to flying through barns and under bridges, barnstormers performed acrobatics and even played tennis on the wings of their biplanes. Everyone was competing to top everyone else.

One barnstormer, a young midwesterner nicknamed Slim, decided to end the contest once and for all. So he executed the ultimate stunt: On May 20–21, he flew across the Atlantic Ocean alone. "Slim," of course, was

FLAPPERS AND FADS (*continued*)
Charles A. Lindbergh, and he instantly became an international celebrity, even among people who had no idea what a barnstormer was.

THE TEAPOT DOME SCANDAL—EVEN MORE BIZARRE THAN ITS NAME

There's no polite way to do this, so, in the interest of conciseness, here goes: President Warren G. Harding didn't have a clue. Following his election, he appointed to sensitive cabinet and government positions a number of his old buddies—now known as the "Ohio Gang"—who, unfortunately, turned out to be among the most

IT'S WASHDAY EVERY DAY IN WASHINGTON

shamelessly corrupt politicians in U.S. history (and you *know* that's saying something). One of the worst was Albert B. Fall, whom Harding had appointed Secretary of the Interior. You might not think that the Department of the Interior would be a good place for a corrupt politician to enrich himself. You'd be wrong.

Not long after he assumed office in 1921, Fall convinced the Secretary of the Navy to turn over to the Interior Department two oil reserve sites—Teapot Dome in Wyoming and Elk Hills in California—which had been established before the war for naval use. Fall then turned around and illegally leased these reserves to private oil companies in exchange for some secret six-digit deposits into Fall's bank account. Now, *that's* corrupt.

Turns out, though, that Fall wasn't quite as clever as he thought. (He would eventually become the first cabinet secretary to be sent to jail.) The whole affair threatened to break to the surface and bring down the Harding administration, disgracing the president in a way that was unprecedented. It looked like it was all over for Harding. But then . . .

GOOD TIMING (PART I)

In addition to good looks, Warren Gamaliel Harding was blessed with good timing. While traveling around the country in the summer of 1923, Harding suffered a heart attack in San Francisco; he seemed to recover, then died suddenly in his hotel room on August 2. Mrs. Harding refused to allow an autopsy, fueling rumors that she had poisoned him to spare him the disgrace of the impending scandal. (Others said it was to avenge her honor; Harding is widely believed to have fathered a child out of wedlock with his young mistress, Nan Britton, while in the White House. Can you imagine the movie this would make?)

The call went out to Plymouth Notch, Vermont, where Vice President Calvin Coolidge was visiting his father. By the light of a kerosene lamp, Coolidge's father, a justice of the peace, swore in his son as the thirtieth president of the United States. Coolidge celebrated by going to sleep. It was good practice; as president, he would sleep an average of eleven hours a day.

President Calvin Coolidge

SILENT (SLEEPING) CAL

Calvin Coolidge was born in Plymouth Notch in 1872. After graduating from Amherst College, he set up a law practice in Northampton, Massachusetts, then entered politics. He was elected to his first office—city councillor of Northampton—at the age of twenty-seven; he rose up through local and state ranks, and was elected governor of Massachusetts in 1918. The following year, Boston was hit by a police strike; Coolidge acted quickly to break the strike, stating: "There is no right to strike against the public safety, by anybody, anywhere, anytime." The action made Coolidge a national hero, especially among antilabor Republicans. A year later, he was drafted as Harding's vice president.

Coolidge was, in many ways, unlike any other man ever to hold the nation's highest office. He was known for his stinginess (he celebrated his first "inauguration" by going down to the local general store and digging a nickel out of his pocket for a bottle of Moxie, leaving his companions to pay for their own) and his reticence; he rarely made speeches, and typically responded to reporters' questions with one- or two-word answers. "If you don't say anything," he once explained, "you can't be called on to repeat it." A woman who once sat next to him at an official dinner informed him that she had bet her friends she could get him to say more than two words to her. "You lose," he replied.

Nevertheless, Coolidge, a conservative Republican, was the right man for the times. In an era when all America seemed intent on amassing fortunes, Coolidge knew the score. "The business of America is business," he said, and made sure that government kept its hand out of the equation. In a decade when Americans seemed to want as little government as possible, they rallied around a president who did as little governing as he possibly could. "America wanted nothing done," said one pundit, "and Coolidge done it." He ran for election in his

---

PRESIDENT COOLIDGE . . . 'NUF SAID

Alice Roosevelt Longworth, TR's daughter, was fond of repeating a snide rumor that Calvin Coolidge had been "weaned on a pickle." Mrs. Longworth once asked Coolidge why he attended so many official parties when they obviously bored him. "Well," Coolidge replied, "a man must eat."

In addition to his taciturnity and parsimoniousness, Coolidge was best known for his fondness for sleep. One afternoon, when a White House staffer shook him during a nap, Coolidge opened his eyes and said, "Is the country still here?" When Coolidge attended an evening performance of the Marx Brothers' show "Animal Crackers," Groucho spotted the president in the audience and announced from the stage, "Isn't it past your bedtime, Calvin?" In 1933, someone told writer Dorothy Parker that Calvin Coolidge had died. "How can they tell?" she responded.

---

own right in 1924, and won easily. Then he went upstairs and took a nap. It was good for the country, he explained; he couldn't be initiating anything if he were asleep.

THE BUSINESS OF AMERICA

If there was one sector of U.S. finance that epitomized the 1920s it was the stock market. Before World War I, the stock market was strictly a gentleman's game, dominated by the likes of J. P. Morgan and Jacob Schiff, men of influence who regarded the market as their domain. That changed in the twenties; it was a decade when everyone—barbers and bankers, builders and barons—was

A SIMPLE MUSIC BOX

Before World War I, radio—then known as wireless telegraphy—was used mostly to transmit Morse code,
point to point. In 1916, a young executive with the
Marconi company sent his boss a memo, proposing that
radio be used to transmit music, talk, and entertainment: "The receiver can be designed in the form of a
simple 'Radio Music Box'. . . . Baseball scores can be
transmitted through the air. . . . [People] could enjoy
concerts, lectures, music, recitals, etc., which may be
going on in the nearest city within their radius. . . . If
only one million . . . families thought well of the idea it
would . . . mean a gross business of about $75 million."
Seventy-five million dollars? You would think that would
make the boss sit up and take notice. But the boss,
Guglielmo Marconi, just ignored the memo. And the
young executive, David Sarnoff, bided his time.

Four years later, his time came. Sarnoff was now in
charge of the Radio Corporation of America, and RCA
started selling its first radio receiver for home use. That
fall, KDKA broadcast the results of the presidential election—a first. And radio sales took off. Sarnoff's estimate
of $75 million in sales soon looked ridiculously small. In
1922, there were only thirty stations broadcasting; by
1923, there were more than five hundred. Between 1923
and 1924, the number of American homes with radios
tripled. Cities and towns and schools and even department stores established stations. For the first time, millions of Americans were exposed to opera and major
league baseball and college lectures and evangelists and
vaudeville comedians and . . . commercials.

scrambling to make a fast fortune, and the stock market
was the fastest game in town. Every day, the newspapers
carried stories of modest little men who had invested a
hundred dollars wisely and walked away millionaires.

In truth, the stock market was anything but a level and stable playing field. It was almost completely devoid of regulation, a situation that opened it to manipulation by greedy operators who bought up certain stocks in bulk to raise the prices, then dumped them after other unsuspecting investors had jumped on the bandwagon, sending the price plummeting, walking away with a fortune in the process. And more and more small investors were getting in on the action because of the margin system, which allowed buyers to "control" large chunks of stock by putting down a very small percentage of the purchase price. It was a system that worked well—as long as the share price continued to rise. If fortunes turned, and prices fell, the small investor faced a huge disaster. But never mind: In the twenties, almost everyone believed that the market would continue to go up and up forever. Even economists were saying so, and the newspapers were happy quote them.

The newspapers gave less coverage to those struggling at the time: Farmers in the Midwest, who were facing their own financial crisis following the removal of World War I–era price supports on wheat and other crops; and labor, which found itself in dire straits, with wages dropping due to more competition from immigrants. The farmers, who had increased their crop production at the behest of Food Administrator Herbert Hoover, were now faced with too much supply and too little demand; prices plummeted. And workers—coal miners, steel workers, truck drivers—found more and more that their only recourse, the labor unions, were becoming increasingly difficult to establish and maintain; bosses, who had always been hostile to unions, now had a powerful ally in the government, which maintained a strict laissez-faire attitude toward business. It would take a colossal crisis to turn things around.

SHUT THAT GOLDEN DOOR

"I lift my lamp beside the golden door," reads "The New Colossus," the poem by Emma Lazarus at the base of the Statue of Liberty in New York Harbor. The golden door, of course, is the gateway to the United States; the statue looks to Europe, and beckons: "Give me your tired, your poor, Your huddled masses, yearning to breathe free. . . ." "The New Colossus," though, was written in 1903 by Emma Lazarus; twenty years later, much of America had grown tired of the "huddled masses," especially certain groups of them.

The backlash against World War I had unleashed some ugly elements onto American society, but none, perhaps, was uglier than the tide of racism and nativism that swept through the country in the 1920s. It pervaded every facet of American life, from big cities to small towns, north and south, east and west. African-Americans who had moved up from the South to work in northern factories during the war now faced race riots in their new, more "tolerant" northern homes. African-American soldiers, having fought in France to "make the world safe for Democracy," now felt entitled to a share of that same promise at home—especially after having experienced a more tolerant, relatively color-blind society in France. But the America they returned to often seemed more determined than ever to keep them down, especially in the South. Jim Crow laws were enforced with new zeal, and the number of lynchings rose sharply. Membership in the Ku Klux Klan hit an all-time high—more than 3 million—in the early and mid-1920s. In addition to African-Americans, the Klan waged war on Catholics, Jews, and immigrants. And they had some help.

After the war, certain segments of popular society became enamored of a new field of "science"—racial studies. Several popular books expounded upon the superior qualities of the "Nordic races" (i.e., people from northern and western Europe) while demeaning and degrading the "darker races" from southern and eastern Europe (not surprisingly, many of these books came out of England, the westernmost point in Europe). These theories found a ready audience among the "polite classes," who were, by and large, composed of the descendants of western and northern Europeans.

The polite classes also made up a large majority of Congress, which turned its eye on the issue of immigration in the early 1920s. Immigration, they decided, was not necessarily undesirable—just immigration from certain "undesirable" countries and regions. As proof, they pointed to the mass deportation of Russian-born "troublemakers" in 1919 (including Emma Goldman and Alexander Berkman), and the case of Nicola Sacco and Bartlomeo Vanzetti, two Italian-born anarchists convicted in 1920 of murdering two people during a robbery of a shoe manufacturer in South Braintree, Massachusetts. (Despite strong evidence of their innocence and pleas for mercy from prominent individuals throughout America and the world, the two were executed on August 23, 1927.)

In 1924, Congress passed—and President Coolidge signed—the Johnson–Reed Immigration Act, which set strict immigration quotas on countries based on their representation in the U.S. population. Sounds reasonable, no?

But the quota—2 percent of said population—was based upon the census of 1890, before most of the "undesirable" countries had started sending immigrants over en masse. Needless to say, the law heavily favored immigrants from northern and western Europe, while countries like Russia and Poland were left out in the cold (or warmth, in the case of southern European nations like Italy and Greece). Of course, they could have had it worse; immigration from Japan was cut off entirely.

These laws would remain on the books for more than forty years.

GOOD TIMING (PART II)

In 1928, Calvin Coolidge made a simple announcement regarding the upcoming presidential election: "I do not choose to run." The GOP said all-righty, and promptly nominated Secretary of Commerce Herbert Hoover, who, you will remember, had made a name for himself by saving Europe from starvation during and after World War I. Coolidge seemed a bit put off by the speed with which the GOP managed to replace him. Little did he know how truly lucky he was, for unbeknownst to him (and the rest of the country), Coolidge had just bailed out of a plane that was about to crash spectacularly, leaving Hoover to take the blame and go down in flames.

SLEEPING OR JUMPING?

On March 4, 1929, Herbert Clark Hoover was sworn in as the thirty-first president of the United States.

Hoover was a Quaker, graduate of Stanford University, a self-made millionaire as a mining engineer. He stood out in the Harding and Coolidge administrations as an honest man (a rare thing in Harding's cabinet) who could, and did, get things done. His energy, intelligence, and compassion were legendary; Franklin D. Roosevelt, who served with him in Woodrow Wilson's administration, once said of Hoover, "I wish I could make him president of the United States. There couldn't be a better one." (Don't you just love history's little ironies?)

President Herbert Clark Hoover

The country, meanwhile, looked like nothing could stop it. True, an economic depression was sweeping across Europe; but in America, things were better than they had ever been. Skyscrapers were going up from New York to California; the highways and roads were covered with automobiles. For a decade, the nation

BARD OF A DECADE

In 1920, Francis Scott Key Fitzgerald was a poor twenty-four-year-old veteran who worked in an auto upholstery shop in his hometown of St. Paul, Minnesota. But later that year, with the publication of his first novel, *This Side of Paradise*, he became an overnight sensation. Fitzgerald went on to become the most celebrated writer of the decade—and, for many, the voice of the Roaring Twenties (which he called "The Jazz Age"). Fitzgerald always seemed to find the words to describe what was happening in the 1920s, even if he didn't find it until much later. In a 1930s essay, "Early Success," he recalled that the decade had begun with great promise, for himself and millions of others:

> *The uncertainties of 1919 were over—there seemed little doubt about what was going to happen—America was going on the greatest, gaudiest spree in history and there was going to be plenty to tell about it.*

Fitzgerald's writing was particularly adept at capturing the world of the very rich, and the money culture that grew out of the strength of the stock market. In his essay, "The Echoes of Jazz," he writes:

> *It was pleasant to be in one's twenties in such a certain and unworried time. Even when you were broke you didn't worry about money, because it was in such profusion around you.*

And Fitzgerald was there, too, when the party was over:

> *It ended . . . because the utter confidence which was its essential prop received an enormous jolt, and it didn't take long for the flimsy structure to settle earthward. . . . It*

BARD OF A DECADE

was borrowed time anyhow—the whole upper tenth of a nation living with the insouciance of grand ducs and the casualness of chorus girls. But moralizing is easy now.

had been having the wildest party in history, paid for, in large part, by the stock market, which seemed to be making just about everyone rich. A few naysayers, like economist John Maynard Keynes, were warning that the party couldn't go on forever; most people just laughed and told Keynes to "23-skidoo." The stock market kept going up, and up, and up, with no end in sight.

The end came on October 24, 1929. Stock prices suddenly started dropping. Speculators were faced with "margin calls"—their obligation to cover the losses with more cash. Many, unable to do so, were forced to sell. As shares flooded the market, the prices dropped more; as prices dropped further, more speculators couldn't make their margin calls, and dumped their shares. Pandemonium broke out on the floor of the New York Stock Exchange. Panic swept the street. By the time trading closed, an astronomical 13 million shares had been sold. Total market values dropped more than $11 billion. On October 28, the market lost another $14 billion. The next day, the market had its worst day ever; 14 million shares traded hands, most for pennies on the dollar, or less.

Thousands of people were ruined; many suffered breakdowns or strokes; some killed themselves, hurling themselves from skyscraper windows. One hotel was said

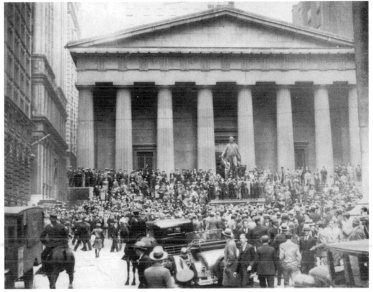

A bewildered and devastated Wall St. crowd, October 1929

to ask nervous guests at its check-in desk whether they wanted a room for sleeping or jumping.

The party was over. The Great Depression was just beginning.

CHAPTER 5

THE THIRTIES
U.S. POPULATION
123,203,000 (1930)

CHEER UP

The next time you get to feeling sorry for your self—you know, your luck stinks, nothing ever goes your way, everything you touch turns to dust, someone up there definitely *doesn't* like you—just remember old Herbert Hoover. I guarantee it'll make you feel better.

Poor President Hoover. Here he was, a brilliant, good-hearted, energetic dynamo who'd worked hard, paid his dues, and, by the by, saved Europe from mass starvation. As secretary of commerce, he'd presided over the greatest stock market boom in history, making everybody rich and happy. Now, at last, he'd worked his way up to the highest office in the land. The greatest showcase in the world for his dynamic, energetic, can-do leadership. He

117

couldn't help but succeed. After all, the last guy had slept twelve hours a day, never cracked a smile, and didn't appear to do very much at all—and almost everyone liked *him* just fine. Yes, it seemed certain that big things were going to happen in the 1930s, and that Herbert Hoover was going to be remembered for them.

They did. And he is. Unfortunately.

Yes, poor President Hoover. In office barely six months, and the bottom falls out of the market. Overnight, what seemed like the richest nation in world history was plunged into what seemed like the worst economic nightmare in history. And maybe it was. Make no mistake: the Great Depression was serious. Very, very serious. It was a worldwide catastrophe. Nothing like it had ever happened before. Not even close.

And Herbert Hoover? He had no idea what he was up against. Not a clue. How could he? Few people had seen it coming. Fewer still knew what it was. And fewer still had even the slightest idea what to do about it.

So you can't really blame Herbert Hoover for not knowing what to do about the Great Depression. The problem was, he didn't even try.

HEY, BUDDY, I'M *STARVING* HERE

The Great Depression broke all the rules. The country had been through economic recessions and even depressions before, usually lasting no more than a year or two. Most had been conquered by the cycle of free-market competition: When business got slack, manufacturers laid off workers, who, in order to avoid homelessness and starvation, lowered their wage demands in order to

BROTHER, CAN YOU SPARE THE TIME?

It would be easy to think of the 1930s as a relentlessly bleak decade, a time when people were too busy worrying where their next meal was coming from to even think about having a good time. While this was often true, it is also true that the 1930s was a time of artistic and creative bounties. Some of the best literature (Ernest Hemingway, F. Scott Fitzgerald, John Steinbeck, William Faulkner), art (George Bellows, John Sloan, Edward Hopper, Grant Wood), and music (George and Ira Gershwin, Duke Ellington, Glenn Miller, Count Basie, Benny Goodman, Louis Armstrong) in U.S. history came out of the 1930s, and in many cases, it wasn't just a select few who were able to appreciate them.

The most popular forms of entertainment in the 1930s—or, at any rate, the most accessible—were movies and radio. Between the two, movies were even more accessible, since going to a movie theater required an investment of a quarter or less, and for that modest price of admission, one often enjoyed an entire day's entertainment. A typical day at a movie theater might include two full-length pictures, several weekly serials and newsreels, and a live floor show. To fill even more seats, theater owners often held ticket-holder raffles, with prizes that included appliances, grocery shopping sprees, and rent money. Most theaters were simple affairs, but many cities also had grand "movie palaces," ornately decorated opera houses that made the people sitting in the seats feel as glamorous as the people on screen. And the movies themselves were dazzling affairs in which people always had cocktails and dined in formal evening wear. And dancers—hundreds of them—performed in elaborately choreographed numbers, forming complex geometric shapes visible only from above. With a few notable exceptions, Depression-era movies were not about the Depression; for the most

---

BROTHER, CAN YOU SPARE THE TIME?
(*continued*)
· ·
part, people went to the theater to escape their woes, and they got what they went for.

Radio required a somewhat larger investment; even the cheapest sets sold for several dollars. But they were well-made and attractive, some even artistic, and they became a focal point in any household as soon as they arrived. Entire extended families—and often neighbors—would gather around the radio at the same time every week to listen to "The Shadow" and "The Green Hornet" and "Jack Armstrong, the All-American Boy" and "The Untouchables" and "Henry Higgins" and "Fibber McGee and Molly" and "The Goldbergs" and "Burns and Allen" and "Amos 'n' Andy," the most popular show of its time. Some of these shows—particularly that last one—might have questionable social value when viewed from a distance of six decades, but there can be no doubt that they brought thousands of hours of entertainment, laughter, and escape to millions of people who badly needed a reprieve.

---

find work. With wages lowered, manufacturers were able to produce products more cheaply, which raised demand, which raised demand for more workers, which raised wages again. It all worked out rather nicely, if you didn't mind the stress of being laid off and scrounging for ill-paying work every few years.

The Great Depression took this cycle and, against all reason, turned it on its head. Workers remained unemployed because manufacturers wouldn't hire them; manufacturers would not hire them because the market for their goods had dried up; the market for their goods had dried up because no one had money to buy them anymore; few people had money to buy them anymore because they remained unemployed.

And it wasn't just industrial workers who lost out. Farmers, who had boosted production during World War I because Herbert Hoover had promised them that "food will win the war," now had more than they knew what to do with—especially since the United States had closed off the massive Russian market during the red scare of 1919, and had never relented. Farm prices, which had been dropping steadily in the 1920s, now plummeted as the average person had less and less money to spend on food. Many farmers struggled to make it through on half the income they had in boom years. Many others were wiped out. Unable to sell their crops, or even work their land anymore, they simply abandoned it, and hit the road in search of work. Those who stayed had their own problems. On land that had been overgrazed, overplanted, and overexploited, the soil was becoming exhausted; when a drought—which would last for three years—hit in 1934, an area of about 150,000 square miles, spreading throughout the Great Plains and into nearly a half-dozen states, was devastated. Once-fertile topsoil literally turned to parched dust and was whipped up by winds into thick "black blizzards" that carried it all the way to the Atlantic Ocean. More than 50 million acres of farmland lost all of their topsoil; another 250 million were severely damaged or nearly destroyed. As a result, 350,000 farmers left their land for dead and fled west, mostly to cities that could scarcely feed the unemployed hordes they already had.

And then there was the trouble with banks. People who had optimistically taken out big loans during the boom of the 1920s suddenly found themselves unable to pay them back. Other people, worried that their banks were about to go belly-up, panicked and stormed the building, demanding their life savings back, in cash, immediately. This kind of hysteria, of course, is contagious, and soon the bank was besieged by a full-fledged "run," the type of riot that actually did cause a few banks to go belly-up, after all. Actually, it was more than a few. Between October 1929 and December 1930, some 1,300 banks went under. Not branches—banks. The kind with dozens of branches, and hundreds of thousands of depositors, every one of them wiped out. (The Federal Reserve System, established under President Wilson in 1913, was ill-prepared and ill-equipped to deal with the crisis, much less prevent it. Not until the Glass-Steagall Act of 1933, which mandated that all twelve Federal Reserve banks insure their deposits, while giving them much greater authority to regulate credit and loans, would the Federal Reserve System have the ability to prevent many banks from failing.)

Through it all, though, President Hoover kept his cool—maybe a little too well. Public officials and private citizens appealed to him by the thousands to help in some way, to bring the immense power of the federal government to bear upon the crisis, to *do* something— anything—to ease the plight of millions of poor and unemployed Americans. But Hoover believed that relief was the responsibility of the private sector, of philanthropists and charities alone, not the government. "The sole function of Government is to bring about a condition of affairs favorable to the beneficial development of private enterprise," he explained. "Prosperity cannot be restored by raids upon the public treasury."

And things just kept getting worse.

JUST WHEN YOU THOUGHT IT COULDN'T GET ANY WORSE . . .

Although 1930 was a bad year, and 1931 was no party either, 1932—now, that was a rough one: 1,616 banks failed that year; 20,000 business firms went bankrupt; the Gross National Product fell to a little more than half its 1929 level; industrial production dropped to just one-third of what it was in 1929. The Dow Jones Industrial Average, which had hit a high of 381.17 on September 3, 1929, fell to just 41.22 on July 28, 1932, an all-time record low. Between 15 million and 17 million people were unemployed; 34 million had no income whatsoever; 21,000 people committed suicide.

Demonstration outside Henry Ford's River Rouge auto factory,
March 7, 1932

Yes, 1932 was a rough one, all right. So rough that on March 7, some 3,000 men, women, and children demonstrated outside Henry Ford's River Rouge auto factory in Dearborn, Michigan, pleading for jobs. Police, called to the scene, tried to break up the crowd. Unsuccessful, they fired into it, instead. Four people were killed. The dead were buried a few days later in a common grave; 30,000 people attended the funeral.

CRIME OF THE CENTURY, THE 1930s NOMINEE

On March 1, 1932, Charles A. Lindbergh, Jr., the nineteen-month-old son of the famous aviator and his wife, Anne Morrow Lindbergh, was kidnapped from his room in the family home near Princeton, New Jersey. Lindbergh soon received a note demanding $50,000 in ransom; he paid it immediately, but his baby was not returned. Instead, on May 12, the child was found, dead, in a remote area of Lindbergh's large estate. The crime touched off one of the largest manhunts in American history. Eventually, police arrested a semi-employed German immigrant named Bruno Richard Hauptmann after finding some of the ransom money in his garage. Hauptmann insisted he was innocent, that he got the money from a former business associate, but to no avail. Despite some credible evidence in his favor, he was convicted (with the help of a rising tide of anti-German prejudice) of the crime and executed on April 3, 1936.

In the wake of the crime, Congress passed the so-called Lindbergh law, making kidnapping a capital offense when the kidnapper crosses state lines in the process of the crime. Lindbergh himself withdrew almost completely from public life. To this day, many experts consider Hauptmann innocent of the crime and his conviction and execution a gross miscarriage of justice.

Yes, 1932 was rough. Really rough. And people couldn't even hope to drink their troubles away: Prohibition, unpopular and unenforceable as it was, was still the law of the land. The year's most popular song began:

> *Once I built a railroad, made it run.*
> *Made it race against time.*
> *Once I built a railroad, now it's done.*
> *Brother, can you spare a dime?*

Times were so tough that Herbert Hoover was even prompted to act, at last. He signed into law a bill creating the Reconstruction Finance Corporation, giving banks and finance companies some $500 million in government funds. Congress passed the Glass-Steagall Act, which allowed the Federal Reserve Bank to expand credit to banks while making more of the federal gold supply available to businesses.

But it was too little, too late. This, after all, was 1932. A mighty bad year. And it was about to get even worse.

MAKING THE WORLD SAFE FOR DEMOCRACY . . . AND $500

In May 1932, U.S. veterans of the Great War began to converge upon Washington, D.C. Within weeks, there would be thousands of them—estimates range between 15,000 and 25,000—many with their families, camped out in parks and on the mall, in front of the Capitol and even the White House.

What did they come for? Oh, about $500.

That was the amount of a bonus Congress had voted to give World War I veterans in 1924, part of what was called the Adjustment Compensation Act. The problem was, the act specified that the bonuses were not to be paid until 1945. The promise of $500 in thirteen years was not enough; the veterans, many of whom had been blinded or maimed in the service of their country, were in dire straits. They needed the money *now*.

Hoover refused. He deplored the marchers—who were now being referred to in the press as the "bonus army"—calling them "Communists and persons with criminal records." Not veterans. Still, the Bonus Army grew. So did their popular support.

On July 28—the same day the stock market hit rock bottom—Hoover decided he'd had enough. He called in the cavalry. Literally.

Armed with bayonets, tear gas, and even tanks, U.S. Army troops advanced on the Bonus Army. Leading the charge was another Great War veteran, now the army's chief of staff; fifty-two-year-old Douglas MacArthur. By Mac-Arthur's side were two more veterans and career soldiers, Majors Dwight D. Eisenhower and George S. Patton.

Army troops burned the protesters' tents and shacks, and forced them to disperse at bayonet point. Two veterans were killed; a three-month-old baby died after inhaling tear gas. A hundred more were injured. Patton led the final charge, burning dozens of tents in his wake, including that of veteran Joseph Angelino of New Jersey. Ironically, during the war, Angelino had won the Distinguished Service Cross for saving Patton's life.

The Bonus Army had been driven off; Hoover had prevailed. But it was a Pyrrhic victory. He was crucified in the press for waging war on decorated veterans, for being insensitive to the veterans' plight, and for prizing his own public image over the welfare of U.S. citizens.

Government attack on the Bonus Army, July 28, 1932

And the election was just three months away.

Meanwhile, the governor of New York was making his own bid for the White House. In accepting the nomination of the Democratic Party that month, he had promised: "I pledge you, I pledge myself, a new deal for the American people." And in a year like 1932, a new deal sounded mighty good.

AN ARISTOCRAT FOR HARD TIMES

The governor of New York had a name that was familiar to voters across the country: Roosevelt. Not Theodore, the late president. This was his fifth cousin, Franklin Delano Roosevelt, known, even in those days, as FDR. In

1905, when FDR was twenty-three and his distant cousin, TR, sat in the White House, FDR married his fourth cousin, Eleanor, who also happened to be TR's niece. Confused? Well, it was a close family.

And it was about as patrician as American families get. Franklin Delano Roosevelt could boast no fewer than a dozen ancestors on the Mayflower; an only child, he was raised on a magnificent estate overlooking the Hudson River in upstate New York, vacationed at another magnificent estate in Nova Scotia, schooled at Groton and Harvard. In other words, not the obvious choice to help the country's rapidly growing poor population make it through the crisis.

But Roosevelt had something of the underdog in him. At Harvard, he had been blackballed by the exclusive social club he had hoped to join; in 1920, after serving as Assistant Secretary of the Navy in the Wilson administration, he ran for vice president on the Democratic ticket, only to be soundly trounced by Warren G. Harding and Calvin Coolidge. The following year, at the age of thirty-nine, Roosevelt contracted "infantile paralysis," or polio. He would never walk unaided again. Nevertheless, he stayed active in politics, and in 1928, when New York's Governor Al Smith resigned to run for president, he convinced Roosevelt to run for the chance to replace him. Smith lost; Roosevelt won.

Now, four years later, he stood before the Democratic National Convention and promised the American people a "new deal." He also promised to repeal Prohibition.

He beat Hoover, of course. It wasn't even close.

ONE HUNDRED DAYS OF NEW DEALIN'
FUN

Whatever Roosevelt meant by a "new deal," he didn't mean just talk. From the moment he was inaugurated, on March 4, 1933—admonishing Americans that "the only thing we have to fear is fear itself"—the man got down to business. He might not have had much of a plan, but he made it up as he went along. The important thing, he said, was to try something; if it failed, try something else. But always try *something.* The first order of business: The crisis with the banks, now reaching national, epidemic proportions.

On March 5, less than twenty-four hours after he became president, Roosevelt declared a four-day bank holiday, starting the next day—a cooling-off period for both customers and the banks themselves (also known, in the child-rearing realm, as a "time-out") during which time

Franklin Delano Roosevelt

there were to be absolutely no dealings in gold, and all banks were to be examined by federal or state authorities, and prohibited to re-open until certified for fiscal fitness. Then, the president did something that would immediately distinguish him in the annals of history: He took to the airwaves. "My fellow Americans, I want to take a few minutes to talk to you about banking," he said to millions of listeners, with the help of a national radio hookup. It was the perfect union of messenger, message, and medium. Radio allowed a president to reach the entire nation in a way never before possible, and no president had ever taken his case so directly to the American people. In the past, issues like the economy and banking were considered too "big" to be handled anywhere but behind closed doors.

Depositors congregate outside the closed doors of the Union Bank of New York City. Photo August 5th, 1931

With this radio address, Roosevelt made the American people feel—for the very first time—as if they, too, were an integral part of the process. The broadcast was so popular—and successful in allaying people's fears and concerns—that Roosevelt decided to make a radio address every week. They soon became known as Roosevelt's "fireside chats," because of the relatively casual tone the president took in addressing his audience. It was a gamble; no president had ever done so before. But, in time, FDR became known for his "fireside chats" as much as for anything else he did in the White House. Many people even hung his picture over their family radio.

On March 9, Roosevelt met with Congress—the first meeting of a legislative marathon that would become known as FDR's "hundred days." In that time, the president and Congress worked together to create more federal programs than at almost any other time in U.S. history.

NEW DEAL ALPHABET SOUP

The president and Congress worked around the clock those first hundred days. Here's what they came up with:

SEC: The Securities and Exchange Commission to regulate and oversee the stock market, where the whole mess began in the first place.

FDIC: The Federal Deposit Insurance Corporation to regulate banks and insure deposits, thus preventing future bank panics.

AAA: The Agriculture Adjustment Administration to implement and maintain farm subsidies, production, and price controls, thus protecting farmers from a whimsical market.

NEW DEAL ALPHABET SOUP (*continued*)

TVA: The Tennessee Valley Authority to bring public power, flood control, and other regional planning services to one of the most rural and impoverished regions of the country.

CCC: The Civilian Conservation Corps to provide unemployed men and women with work on environmental projects.

CWA: The Civil Works Administration to provide unemployed men and women with work on rural and urban projects.

FERA: The Federal Emergency Relief Administration to help out men and women not aided by the CCC or the CWA.

PWA: The Public Works Administration creating even more jobs for men and women, working on public infrastructure projects such as building dams, power plants, highways, and housing projects.

NRA: The National Recovery Administration was a program to implement price and wage controls through the cooperation of labor, business, and government.

NIRA: The National Industrial Recovery Act was a far-reaching program that encouraged the organization of unions and guaranteed workers the right to collective bargaining.

Not bad for a few months' work, eh?

PUTTING YOUR TRUST IN BRAINS (OR VICE VERSA)

No doubt about it, FDR was a pretty smart guy. After all, he came up with some of the most innovative government initiatives and programs in U.S. history, all in the service of conquering what might have been the world's worst financial catastrophe. But he did have some help.

As governor in 1932, Roosevelt was hustling to win the Democratic nomination for president, and his legal counsel, Samuel Rosenman, suggested that he put together a think tank to devise novel ways of setting the economy right. Roosevelt called upon some of the best-known thinkers of the era, including a trio of professors from Columbia University—Adolf Berle, Jr.; Raymond Moley; and Rexford G. Tugwell—as well as another from Harvard Law School, a Viennese immigrant named Felix Frankfurter (Roosevelt would eventually appoint Frankfurter to the Supreme Court). This group of advisers eventually became known to the general public as Roosevelt's "brain trust." That term was used as a compliment by New Deal supporters, who appreciated Roosevelt's bringing such massive brain power to bear upon the struggle to beat the Depression; it was also used disparagingly by FDR's opponents, who conjectured that intellectuals and government did not mix, unless your objective was socialism or communism.

Though Roosevelt soon came to rely quite heavily upon his "brain trusters," ultimately, it was he alone who decided which of their disparate suggestions became policy. The brain trusters themselves were a diverse lot, and were rarely in agreement about anything; the commander in chief used that to his advantage, picking and choosing his initiatives from the mixture. Many of his agencies and initiatives were actually a combination of two or more individual ideas.

WHOOPS! FORGOT ABOUT THAT THIRD BRANCH OF GOVERNMENT

Roosevelt's hundred days' programs breezed through Congress—not surprising, since the 1932 elections had also swept new Democratic majorities into both the House of Representatives and the Senate. They were also, not surprisingly, very popular with the American public. They actually did manage to stabilize prices, wages, and farm production, while creating jobs for millions of people.

On the other hand, with their radical redefinition of the government's role in overseeing and even influencing the economy and business they also managed to anger an awful lot of conservatives, including about a half dozen who just happened to be sitting on the Supreme Court at the time. The Court declared a number of the programs unconstitutional, including the extremely popular NIRA, the NRA, and the AAA, which had brought desperately needed relief to the Midwest. Other critics attacked programs like the CCC and the PWA as "make-work" scams, which paid people money to do work that was unnecessary. Meanwhile, forces on the left side of the political spectrum were agitating for the president to do even more.

In 1935, Roosevelt unveiled his second phase of the New Deal. It included the Works Progress Administration (WPA), one of FDR's most memorable and controversial programs. The WPA created work and jobs for hundreds of thousands of people, everyone from unskilled laborers to writers, historians, artists, and photographers. Also included were two programs that continue to have a powerful impact on U.S. society to this day: the Social Security Act, which established pensions for the elderly, welfare for children and the disabled, and insurance for the unemployed; and the National Labor Relations Act (a.k.a. the Wagner Act), which restored labor organizing and collective bargaining provisions from the now defunct NIRA. The new programs were so popular that Roosevelt easily defeated his Republican opponent, Alf Landon, in the election a year and a half later. The Democrats cleaned up, too, gaining huge majorities in both the House (331 to 89) and the Senate (76 to 16). The country was still in trouble (as FDR would state in his second inaugural address, "I see one third of a nation ill-housed, ill-clad, ill-nourished") but the president was at the height of his powers.

Still, his problems continued with the largely conservative Supreme Court—composed, at that time, of nine white men, every one of them more than sixty years old. Roosevelt grew increasingly frustrated with a judiciary that (as he saw it) was just maliciously knocking down everything he had worked so hard to accomplish. "The Court," he complained, "has been acting not as a judicial body, but as a policy-making body." So he conceived of a scheme: He would "pack" the Supreme Court, expanding the bench from nine justices to as many as fifteen and filling the new seats with pro-New Deal justices. In other words, if he couldn't get a sympathetic majority out of the Court, he would just make one up for himself. Oh, yes, and for the rest of the country, too.

On February 5, 1937, Roosevelt informed his cabinet of his plan. Ostensibly, it would streamline the entire federal judiciary, but at its heart was a proposal to expand the Supreme Court unless all the justices over the age of seventy promptly retired. Needless to say, this plan proved to be somewhat . . . controversial—to say the least.

Critics attacked Roosevelt for disregarding the Constitution, trying to upset the balance of power by making the Executive branch more powerful than the Legislative or Judiciary. They called him everything from a dictator to a maniac. His friends weren't much kinder. In fact, many of them became enemies.

Roosevelt backed off—sort of. Instead, he got Congress to pass the Supreme Court Retirement Act, which allowed justices to retire at seventy with full pay. In other words, a bribe instead of blackmail. There were no takers.

But what seemed at the moment like a defeat for Roosevelt soon proved to be something else entirely. That spring, the Court abruptly changed course, and began ruling that Roosevelt's latest New Deal initiatives—including Social Security and the National Labor Relations Act—were, in fact, *constitutional.* Roosevelt's retreat, it seems, won him the victory he had sought.

HARD TIMES, BAD SIGNS

After he won re-election in 1936, Roosevelt decided to take on a new task: balancing the budget. Doing so after four years of vastly increased federal spending would be no easy task. The government would have to tighten its belt—meaning, simply, that the people would have to do so, too.

But the country wasn't ready yet, and in the fall of 1937, it plunged into a severe recession that lasted more than a year. At first, Roosevelt, loathe to increase spending, attacked the recession with words, tearing into an old and easy target: monopolies. While this may have won the chief a popularity contest or two, it didn't really help the country. By the following spring, FDR set aside his new objective, and returned to the old one: basic human relief. This meant an increase in federal spending—5 billion dollars' worth. One of the architects of this new spending spree was economist John Maynard Keynes, who had predicted the stock market crash and, six years later, had written the revolutionary book *The General Theory of Employment, Interest, and Money*. The book's main thesis—that large-scale, long-term government intervention in the economy (and big government spending) was the best way to achieve and maintain high employment levels and lasting prosperity—would be a guiding principle in presidential administrations for the next half century; and Roosevelt's spring 1938 initiative would mark the beginning of what would become known as "Keynesian economics." And the initiative's culmination that year, the Fair Labor Standards Act, would be revolutionary in its own way, establishing a national minimum wage and a maximum work week.

But by 1938, it was also becoming clear, even to Roosevelt, that the government alone couldn't spend its way out of the Depression. A major trauma like the Great Depression could only be overcome by another major trauma.

As fate would have it, at that moment another major

trauma was, indeed, looming on the horizon. In Europe, German dictator Adolf Hitler had already annexed Austria and the Sudetenland region of Czechoslovakia, and was gearing up to invade Poland; in Asia, Japan had invaded Manchuria and was plunging deeper and deeper into China. In his 1938 State of the Union address, Roosevelt had taken a moment out of pondering the economy to state that the nation needed to beef up its defense capability; in 1939, he dedicated most of the address to foreign affairs, calling on all democracies to prepare for what lay ahead. What lay ahead was a war, the greatest in world history. Roosevelt would guide that nation through that, too. And when it was over, his nation would be the richest and most powerful on earth, though he would not live to see it happen.

![CHAPTER 6]

THE FORTIES

U.S. POPULATION:
131,669,275

IT WAS THE WORST OF TIMES, IT WAS THE WORST OF TIMES

The year 1940 was not exactly a great one for America. The country was still caught in the viselike grip of the Great Depression, and the war that was raging throughout Europe and Asia was scaring the heck out of just about everybody here. Then again, we definitely had it better than, say, western and central Europe, most of which had been overrun and occupied by the Nazis, and China, much of which had been overrun and occupied by the Japanese. (Fascist dictator Benito Mussolini's Italy, which had flexed its muscle against Ethiopia in the previous decade, was the third party to the Berlin-Tokyo-Rome Axis, but couldn't lend the Axis' war effort much more than warm bodies and moral support. Italy occupied Albania in 1939, but when Mussolini's army tried to invade Greece the following year, it took a serious beating from the Greek army and had to be bailed out by Hitler's *Wehrmacht*.)

And, as if being conquered just for the sake of acquiring more territory, natural resources, and power wasn't bad enough, the defeated suffered a great deal at the hands of the German Army and Nazi officials, who did evil things like deport and execute large segments of the population, used innocent civilians as guinea pigs in grotesque "medical experiments," and destroyed ancient national treasures and landmarks just for the fun of it. The Holocaust, Hitler's attempt to systematically annihilate the Jewish people, would not begin in earnest until late 1941 and early 1942, more than two years into the war; nevertheless, in a little more than three years, Hitler and his killing machine would manage to murder 6 million Jews, roughly 86 percent of Europe's Jewish population.

In some wars, it is possible to respect and even admire your opponent. This was not one of those wars. By 1940, it had become obvious to most Americans that the United States was going to get involved sooner or later. Many Americans were in favor of U.S. intervention on the side of the Allies; the most important advocate of this position was the president of the United States, Franklin Delano Roosevelt. Before we deal with that, though, let's take a quick look at the folks on the other side of the issue.

AMERICA FIRST, LAST, AND ONLY

It's important to note that a majority of Americans who opposed U.S. entry into World War II were genuine, honest-to-goodness pacifists who were war-weary from the last time around, and saw no reason why the

United States had to assume the responsibility for making sure that the rest of the planet behaved themselves. But it's also fair to note that some of the most vocal 1940s noninterventionists—also known, back then, as "isolationists"—weren't really opposed to America entering the war, so much as they abhorred the idea of America entering the war *on the side of the Allies.* Yes, it's an ugly thought, but true. There were people in this country who liked Hitler and the Nazis, and agreed with their ideas. Some were nationalistic Germans or Americans of German descent; and others were, well, just plain twisted.

Into the former category fell two linked organizations, the German-American Bund and its paramilitary arm, the Silver Shirts, modeled after the Brownshirts of Hitler's SA organization. The Bund was led by Fritz Kuhn, a follower of Hitler's who used the ugly anti-German prejudice of the World War I era to galvanize his group in the 1930s. Kuhn preached a mixture of anti-Semitism, Aryan racial supremacy, and anti-immigrant nativism (unless, of course, those immigrants were from Germany or other "Nordic" countries). Ironically, the Bund, which at its peak had some eight to ten thousand members nationwide, was headquartered in New York, by then the most Jewish city in the world. They staged parades up Third Avenue in the largely German Manhattan neighborhood of Yorkville, hosted "camps" on Long Island and in New Jersey, and organized rallies that, as often as not, degenerated into violence. Kuhn and the Bund, though, were rarely successful in attracting members who were not German, and were shunned by most German-Americans, as well. Kuhn was eventually convicted of embezzlement and sent to prison, and the government shut down Bund headquarters in December 1941.

More prominent were a handful of national figures who exercised their powerful influence and sometimes hid their pro-Nazi leanings behind less odious-sounding political agenda. Among these were Charles Lindbergh, the famed 1920s aviator, who was a proponent of Hitler's racial ideas (he once issued a warning to American Jews that they would pay dearly should they "goad" America into entering the war against the Nazis; had test-flown *Luftwaffe* aircraft for Hermann Goering in the 1930s, a favor for which Goering gave Lindbergh a medal), and in 1940 became a charter member and ardent spokesman for the isolationist "America First" Committee (an organization that was not, it should be stated, overtly anti-Semitic or pro-Nazi, though some of its members most certainly were); Father Charles Coughlin, an immensely popular radio priest of the 1930s, who used the medium to preach anti-Semitism and isolationism and express support for Hitler and Mussolini; and Henry Ford, who had published an anti-Semitic newspaper in the 1920s and kept a picture of Hitler on his desk (Hitler, it is said, returned the favor by keeping a picture of Ford on *his* desk).

Ironically, while the Catholic Church ended Father Coughlin's radio career in 1942, the war proved a boon for both Ford, who profited immensely from government armaments contracts, and Lindbergh, who heroically flew fifty combat missions against Japan and emerged from the conflict a hero yet again.

LEND-LEASE—WHATEVER, THEY'RE ALL YOURS

In addition to Lindbergh, "America First" charter members included *Chicago Tribune* publisher Robert R. McCormick, Chairman Robert E. Wood of Sears, Roebuck, and a handful of U.S. Senators, including Burton K. Wheeler, William E. Borah, and Gerald P. Nye. With Lindbergh as a figurehead, the movement grew, and within a year there were more than 450 chapters, and hundreds of thousands of members. Not exactly an insignificant number.

The other side, however, had President Franklin D. Roosevelt in its camp, and FDR was quite a trump card. Not only did he have the desire to find a way to aid the Allies, he had the energy to try, and the power to succeed.

Roosevelt used his fireside chats to win sympathy for the vanquished Europeans and the valiant British, struggling under the intrepid leadership of Prime Minister Winston Churchill to remain free in the face of the sinister, nigh-overwhelming threat of the Nazi war machine, even as the *Luftwaffe* waged its ruthless *blitz* on the island, bombing English cities, towns, and ports for nine months, dropping nearly 60,000 tons of explosives and killing more than 40,000 Britons. Meanwhile, he pursued—not always overtly—a policy of making the United States the "arsenal of Democracy," responsible for establishing and maintaining a lifeline that shuttled food and arms to the besieged nations that needed them desperately. In 1940, Roosevelt allowed himself to be "drafted," and shattered precedent by running for a third term, assuring the public that he could get them through a war just as he had gotten them through the Depression (which was still going full force). Paradoxically, he also assured voters that he would not send American boys to fight overseas. Despite these gaps in logic, Roosevelt won 55 percent of the popular votes and beat his Republican opponent, a little-known Indiana businessman named Wendell Willkie, 449 electoral votes to 82. That fall, he also pushed through Congress the Selective Service Law, reviving the military draft for the first time since 1918. More than 16 million men registered for the draft as a result.

These victories under his belt, Roosevelt leaned on Congress to pass the Lend-Lease Act. Lend-Lease gave the president the authority to send arms and other war materiel (paid for by American tax dollars, of course) to "any country whose defense the President deems vital to the defense of the United States," free of charge. Needless to say, Lend-Lease was vehemently opposed by many isolationists, including Senator Robert A. Taft of Ohio, son of the late president and the most powerful Republican in Washington, who lamented that the act would allow the president to "carry on a kind of undeclared war all over the world." Nevertheless, Congress passed Lend-Lease on March 11, 1941, and almost immediately, the U.S. started shipping arms to Britain, China, Brazil, and the Soviet Union, to which it took a tortuous shipping route through the Arctic Circle that became legendary as "the Murmansk run." But opposition to Roosevelt's interventionist leanings never let up in Congress.

Never, that is, until the Japanese bombed the U.S. naval base at Pearl Harbor, Hawaii, on the morning of December 7, 1941.

A Japanese bomber on a run over Pearl Harbor, Hawaii, December 7, 1941

INFAMY, AND THEN SOME

Now, there's some controversy surrounding the Japanese attack on Pearl Harbor, specifically surrounding the president, what he knew, and when he knew it. The traditional story is that FDR was as shocked by the attack as everyone else the country. Some historians, however, claim that Roosevelt knew Japanese carriers were ominously approaching Pearl Harbor as early as December 2, but that he said and did nothing in the belief that such a surprise attack was the only way he could draw the United States into the war with the overwhelming support of the American people. However it happened—and, let's face it, we'll never *really* know for sure—a few facts are undeniable. At 7:55 A.M. on the morning of December 7, 1941, the first wave of some 360 Japanese airplanes attacked Pearl Harbor, dropping bombs and

NOT QUITE INVULNERABLE

If the Japanese attack on Pearl Harbor killed any American notion, it was the one that held that this country was protected by two oceans from enemy attack. Throughout the war that followed, U.S. civilians in the Civil Defense searched the skies for enemy bombers, and U.S. cities and towns had frequent air-raid drills that often included total blackouts. (During this period, the windows of the New York Public Library's reading room were blackened to make the building less conspicuous in the event of a nighttime enemy air raid, lending the room the eerie dark light that it maintains to this day.)

While all this might, in retrospect, seem a little comical, the idea of an enemy invasion was not as ridiculous as it appears today. The Japanese did, in fact, capture two Alaskan islands, and on February 23, 1942, an oil refinery near Santa Barbara, California, was hit by shells from a Japanese submarine. Four months later, Japanese subs shelled several coastal towns in Oregon. In September, a Japanese airplane—launched by catapult from a submarine—dropped incendiary bombs near Brookings, Oregon, in the hopes of starting forest fires. The Japanese also launched balloons carrying incendiary bombs, which were carried over the Pacific toward the U.S. by the wind; one actually started a fire that killed several people in Oregon. On the East Coast, the U.S. Coast Guard sank German U-boats off the coasts of Rhode Island, Massachusetts, and New York; and in June 1942, U-boats smuggled eight German spies onto beaches in Long Island and Florida. They were all captured quickly and six were executed.

The war hit home in other ways, too. Civilians were encouraged—even mandated—to scour their attics, basements, and garages for scrap metal and rubber, essential to the war effort. Since nickel was also essential, U.S. five-cent pieces were, for several years, com-

NOT QUITE INVULNERABLE (*continued*) . . . .
posed largely of silver. In 1943, all U.S. pennies were
made of zinc, because copper, too, was an essential
metal. Meat, sugar, and gasoline were strictly rationed,
and such commonplace items as nylon stockings, automobiles, and radios stopped being made for a time, as
the industries that manufactured them shifted their efforts toward war materiel. Most Americans were satis-
fied to make the sacrifices for the war effort, even
proud. But naturally, a thriving black market for rationed
goods also developed.

spraying the base and ships with machine-gun fire. A
second wave of attack began an hour later. By 9:45, more
than 2,300 U.S. servicemen were dead, and thousands
more had been wounded; nineteen U.S. ships—battle-
ships, destroyers, and cruisers—had been sunk or severely damaged, including every battleship in the base
except the U.S.S. *Pennsylvania*, which survived only because it was in dry dock. Only the base's three aircraft
carriers—which were all, coincidentally, out at sea on
training maneuvers—were spared. The American Pacific
Fleet had been crippled; nothing like it had ever happened in U.S. history. That same afternoon, Japanese
planes bombed Clark Field, the largest and most important U.S. air base in the Philippines. When the smoke
cleared, half of the American Far East Air Force was
destroyed in that attack.

Whether or not you believe that FDR knew about Pearl
Harbor in advance, the Japanese attack did not exactly
come out of the blue. Relations between the United
States and Japan had been insecure since 1905, when
Theodore Roosevelt, distrustful of Japan, intervened to

end the Russo-Japanese War before Japan could win an all-out victory and seized huge chunks of Pacific territory. The United States had been careful to keep Japan in check, and weaken it economically, at the end of World War I, and even had an arrangement (the extremely ill-named "Gentlemen's Agreement" of 1907) designed to minimize Japanese immigration to the States. Was American fear and distrust of Japan partially racist in origin and nature? You bet it was. Still, Japan wasn't exactly on its best behavior.

On July 7, 1937, Japan had used an extremely flimsy pretext to invade China. Roosevelt responded swiftly and aggressively, condemning the attack and making it clear that diplomatic relations between the United States and Japan were at risk. Japan attempted to mollify Roosevelt, but continued plunging deeper and deeper into Chinese territory. Relations deteriorated and, by 1940, Japan sought to strengthen its sense of security by joining the Fascist Axis of Germany and Italy. Roosevelt responded by placing an embargo on Japan, refusing to sell it any more iron, steel, scrap metal, or gasoline. When Japan invaded Indochina in July 1941, Roosevelt stopped selling Japan oil altogether, banned it from using the Panama Canal, and, worst of all, froze all Japanese assets in the United States. That fall, American and Japanese officials met in Washington on several occasions, but failed to iron out their differences, or even to come close. By December 3, Japanese consulates in the United States were ordered to burn their secret documents. By then, of course, the decisions had already been made.

On December 8, FDR addressed a special joint session of Congress. Calling the previous day "a date which will live in infamy," he asked Congress to declare war on

Japan, which it did without hesitation. In fact, of a total of 471 senators and representatives, only one—Jeanette Rankin of Montana—voted against declaring war. Rankin, at least, was consistent; she had also voted against the United States entering World War I in 1917.

Three days later, Hitler and Mussolini declared war on the United States. Secretly, Roosevelt was relieved; now America could enter the war against the Nazis as a defensive measure, sparing him the task of seeking a formal declaration of war on Germany and Italy.

MORE BAD NEWS

Oh, the days and months following Pearl Harbor were bleak, indeed. On December 10, 1941, the Japanese Army invaded the Philippines, a U.S. military stronghold for more than four decades; that same day, they took the Pacific island of Guam, a U.S. territory. On December 23, the Japanese overran Wake Island, another U.S. territory; on Christmas Day, they took the British crown colony of Hong Kong. And on January 2, 1942, the Japanese took Manila, capital of the Philippines; with no place else to go, the badly out-gunned and out-numbered U.S. troops were forced to withdraw to the Bataan Peninsula, their backs, literally, to the water. Commander Douglas MacArthur set up headquarters on Corregidor, an island fortress in Manila Bay, and U.S. soldiers rallied to raise their own morale, but their position was hopeless. Two months later, after the Allied fleet was all but destroyed during a naval battle in the Java Sea, MacArthur was ordered to leave Corregidor and withdraw to Australia, lest he be captured by the

Japanese. As he departed, on March 11, he turned to the troops he was leaving behind under the command of General Jonathan Wainwright, and declared, "I shall return." The troops cheered, of course, just hoping it would be soon.

As it happened, it would take three years for MacArthur to make good on his promise, and by then, the troops he left behind were long gone, having all been captured or killed by the Japanese. On April 9, the last U.S. forces on Bataan—76,000 troops in all—surrendered to the enemy. (They were forced to march more than a hundred miles to prison camps, under brutal conditions; thousands died along the way. The episode is now remembered as the Bataan Death March.) By spring, the Japanese had captured Wainwright and his remaining troops, along with Thailand, Indochina, Singapore, Borneo, the Dutch East Indies, and a chain of Pacific islands known as the Solomons.

Exuberant with their string of victories, the Japanese now planned to knock the Allies out of the war by invading Australia, Hawaii, and, if necessary, Alaska and the west coast of the United States. Across America, a tide of panic slowly started to rise.

INFAMY, AMERICAN-STYLE

No doubt about it: The war came as a tremendous boon to millions of less fortunate Americans. Huge defense contracts, coupled with a shortage of manpower (thanks to the war and the draft) meant that manufacturers had a lot of jobs to fill and few people with which to fill them. Naturally, this led to a steep rise in wages; it created millions of jobs for women, who, by and large, had worked only in clerical positions, if at all, and for African-Americans, hundreds of thousands of whom left their low-paying, subsistence-level agricultural jobs down South and migrated to the factories of the urban North. In the years and decades that would follow the war, these new opportunities and experiences would become the foundation of revolutionary new social movements, and the kind of change that would have a positive impact on millions of lives in America and around the world.

For some Americans, however, the war brought anything but opportunity and advancement.

On December 7, 1941, there were no less than 127,000 people of Japanese ancestry living in America, most of them in California and other western states. Many had roots that went back generations in the United States, and a majority were model citizens, despite the fact that in many states they were prohibited by law from voting or owning land. Nevertheless, after Pearl Harbor, suspicion and fear of the "yellow peril" swept across America, bolstered by rumors of a Japanese-American conspiracy to sabotage the U.S. war effort from within. The resultant panic led to one of the most disgraceful chapters in modern U.S. history.

On February 19, 1942, President Roosevelt issued Order 9066; as a result, more than 100,000 Japanese-Americans—many native-born, two-thirds of them U.S. citizens—were rounded up and relocated to internment camps in remote areas throughout the West. Most were given just forty-eight hours to sell or otherwise dispose of their homes and property; all told, Japanese-Americans lost an estimated $400 million worth of property in the process.

The camps themselves were comparable to medium-security prisons. "Internees" were housed in cramped tarpaper shacks heated by ancient, dirty coal stoves. Bathroom facilities were inadequate, and the food was just plain bad. Worse, still, was the humiliation suffered by the internees—kept under constant guard by armed soldiers—who had committed no crime other than being Japanese. Only *nisei*, or American-born Japanese, were allowed to hold any position of authority in the camps. Families were often split up. Nevertheless, when offered the opportunity to form their own unit to fight the Japanese in the Pacific, 1,200 *nisei* internees volunteered. Their units proved to be among the most highly decorated of the war.

Roosevelt did not rescind the order until 1944, and the last camps did not close until 1945. It would take decades before the government would even begin to reimburse former internees for their losses, and until 1988 for Congress to award restitution payments to some 60,000 surviving internees.

THE TURNING POINT

And now, back to the spring of 1942.

The Japanese, seemingly unstoppable, had set their sights on Australia and Hawaii. A daring April 18 bombing raid on Tokyo, led by Major General James Doolittle—along with a U.S. naval victory in the Coral Sea that May, in which the Americans blocked the Japanese from landing at Port Moresby, New Guinea—lifted American spirits but only heightened the Japanese high command's desire to defeat America and make it hurt. They sent their fleet toward Midway Island, a U.S. stronghold 1,500 miles northwest of Hawaii. The plan was to catch the U.S. Pacific Fleet off guard and destroy it, leaving Hawaii defenseless.

It almost worked, too. But the Japanese hadn't counted on one thing: We broke their code. *We*, in this case, was a team of brilliant cryptographers, working around the clock. And *their code* was "Purple," one of the most complicated ciphers in history. No small feat.

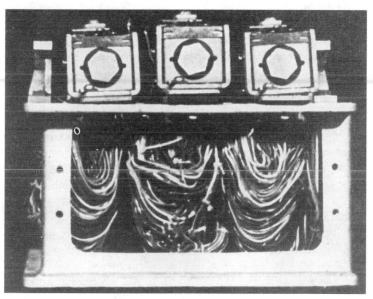

Machine used to break the code "Purple"

And no small payoff. On June 4, 1942, it was the Americans who caught the Japanese fleet off guard, sinking four—count 'em, four—Japanese aircraft carriers. The Japanese had gone to Midway to destroy the U.S. fleet and open the door to Hawaii and Australia; they left with their own fleet in ruins, with Hawaii and Austra-

THE REALLY WILD BLUE YONDER

The airplane, of course, first saw combat in World War I. In that earlier war, however, planes were used primarily to scout battlefield positions and harass enemy troops; they were not major weapons of war. Flying those old *Sopwiths* and *Fokkers* was dangerous, to be sure, but it was also glamorous, a mission surrounded by the aura of panache with a hint of fun about it, too. A top air ace might have a few dozen enemy casualties to his credit.

Between the two world wars, major technological advances were made in aviation; planes shed their second and third wings, grew larger and longer, and were capable of flying much higher, much faster, much farther. By the 1930s, it was becoming obvious to those who contemplated such things that the airplane would inevitably be a major weapon in the next war—perhaps the major weapon. Britain and Germany poured immense amounts of money and manpower into building air forces. So did the United States. In 1935, America began building and flying the B-17 bomber, nicknamed the Flying Fortress, a remarkably sturdy plane that could carry three tons of bombs, travel 1,100 miles without refueling, and had a top speed of 220 miles per hour. It also packed a dozen .50-caliber machine guns. There was nothing else like it in the air.

Immediately, the B-17 and other planes (including the B-24, which debuted a few years later) changed the rules of warfare. Planes could now carry enough bombs to do major strategic damage, and they could travel far enough to strike deep in the heart of enemy territory. No longer a novelty, they were now indispensable. War itself was no longer confined to the battlefields; now the killing could be carried anywhere, even to otherwise peaceful cities and towns hundreds of miles from the front. It was the beginning of modern "total" warfare.

THE REALLY WILD BLUE YONDER
(*continued*)
Hitler's success in swiftly conquering western Europe was due, in large part, to his air force, the *Luftwaffe*, which destroyed most enemy planes before they even got off the ground.

During the battle of Britain, England (and thus the Alliance) was saved from conquest by the *Hurricane* and the *Spitfire*, the legendary British fighters, which were so well-designed and made that the Royal Air Force shot down two German planes for every one it lost. And by the war's end, the B-17 and other Allied bombers had destroyed most of Germany's industrial and transportation resources. Still the cost was high; nearly 10,000 U.S. bombers were shot down (another 8,000 were damaged irreparably), along with some 8,400 fighters, and more than 60,000 U.S. airmen were killed or wounded. Costs for the enemy were even higher. A lone bomber could kill thousands on the ground in a single mission; firebomb raids near the war's end killed 135,000 people in Dresden and 124,000 in Tokyo.

lia safe for the remainder of the war, and with America gaining control of the Pacific, starting down a slow and deadly course to drive the Japanese off the islands they had taken so hurriedly (including Attu and Kiska, two of the outermost islands in the Aleutians, off Alaska). The war in the Pacific would rage on for three more years, and the Allies would lose hundreds of thousands of men; but beginning on June 4, 1942, the Japanese war machine would always be on the defensive, always struggling to hold their ground, never even considering taking new ground. For them, it was the beginning of a long, bloody end.

MEANWHILE, ON THE OTHER SIDE OF THE WORLD . . .

The war against Germany took a little longer to get off the ground, so to speak. Then again, in 1941, the United States didn't have much of an army, and it takes a little time to put together the kind of fighting force that can conquer a hemisphere. Germany and Japan had been putting theirs together for about a decade. The United States had to play one mean game of catch-up. Fortunately, playing catch-up just happened to be something Americans did very, very well. By July 4, 1942, U.S. pilots were flying bombing missions over Europe. By January 1943, U.S. troops were fighting in Italy and North Africa; after some initial defeats (most notably in North Africa, at the hands of Hitler's greatest general, Erwin Rommel, a.k.a "Desert Fox"), both campaigns were ultimately successful, and the Allies were soon at work planning a large-scale invasion on the European continent, to take place on the coast of France. The operation was assigned the code name Overlord, although it soon became known, popularly, as D-Day. The man in charge of planning Overlord was a virtual unknown. The fifty-three-year-old former assistant to the Army Chief of Staff, a veteran of the First World War who had helped drive the bonus army out of Washington in 1932, was appointed, a decade later, commander in chief of the Allied forces in the invasion of North Africa: Dwight David Eisenhower.

In 1942, President Roosevelt had placed Eisenhower in charge of all U.S. forces fighting in the European theater of operations. The choice surprised almost everyone (including Eisenhower himself); at the time, the army's best-known and most highly regarded officer was

SOME OTHER AMERICAN LEADERS OF WORLD WAR II

Admiral Chester W. Nimitz (1885–1966): Nimitz took command of the Pacific Fleet after Pearl Harbor; hero for planning the successful battles of Coral Sea, Midway, and Guadalcanal. By war's end, he was fleet commander of the largest navy in the world.

General George S. Patton (1885–1945): After commanding U.S. forces in North Africa and Sicily, he was placed in charge of the U.S. Third Army in Europe. His troops spearheaded the drive through France and into Germany. A superb soldier, Patton had trouble off the battlefield; in October 1945, he was relieved of his command, and in December he was killed after being struck by a jeep.

General Omar Bradley (1893–1981): A veteran of World War I, Bradley commanded the U.S. First Army in Europe during the invasion of Normandy, and later the U.S. Twelfth Army as it headed eastward, fighting toward Germany. After the war, Bradley was promoted to five-star general and made the first chairman of the Joint Chiefs of Staff.

General Jonathan M. Wainwright (1883–1953): Left behind to command U.S. troops in the Philippines after MacArthur's evacuation, Wainwright surrendered Corregidor to the Japanese and survived both the Bataan Death March and more than two years of imprisonment in a brutal Japanese POW camp. Emaciated and weak, he nonetheless attended the formal Japanese surrender ceremony on September 2, 1945.

General Leslie R. Groves (1896–1970): Assigned, in 1942, to oversee the Manhattan District of the Army Corps of Engineers, Groves was responsible for coordinating the massive Manhattan Project, the program to develop the world's first atomic bomb.

General George C. Marshall, the army's chief of staff, and it was taken for granted that Marshall would lead the invasion of Europe. But at the last moment, Roosevelt decided that Marshall was more valuable in Washington than overseas. Instead, FDR appointed Eisenhower, a general who was not well-known but who had, during army training exercises in 1941, earned a reputation as a superb tactician. Now, Eisenhower—promoted to brigadier general only the year before—was placed in command of an army of 3 million men (drawn from more than a dozen countries), the largest in history. His job was to plan an invasion of massive proportions.

Planning took almost two years. On June 6, 1944, some 5,000 ships and 10,000 planes helped 176,000 Allied troops—the largest invasion force in history—land on

The invasion of Normandy, France, June 6, 1944

nearly a half dozen beaches in Normandy, France. Their arrival had been prepared for by two U.S. airborne divisions, the 82nd and 101st, who had dropped in by parachute and glider the night before. The invaders met fierce resistance, being cut down by German artillery and machine-gun fire, and casualties ran high; nearly a thousand U.S. troops, under the command of General Omar Bradley, fell on Omaha Beach alone. But the Allies took ground and held it, including the town of Cherbourg, and by nightfall, there were 150,000 Allied soldiers in Normandy. Within a week, the Allies had landed more than 300,000 soldiers, along with 100,000 tons of supplies and 50,000 vehicles. There would be some tough fighting in the months ahead. There was, for example, the Battle of the Bulge in December, in which the German army stunned the Allies and broke through their lines with a massive counterattack, leaving the badly outnumbered 101st Airborne Division stranded in Bastogne, where it was nearly done in by both the *Wehrmacht* and the bitter cold. (Advised by the Germans to surrender the 101st Airborne, Major General Anthony C. McAuliffe refused with a one word reply: "Nuts!") But from D-Day on, the steady march of Allied troops toward Berlin meant that the total defeat of Nazi Germany was only a matter of time.

Of course, a lot of the credit also belongs to the Soviet Union, which had been at war with Germany for three years already, and had tied up as much as two-thirds of Hitler's army, sustaining extremely heavy losses and inflicting the same. Nevertheless, from the time it became apparent to the Allies that Germany would ultimately fall, combating the Nazis had to share Roosevelt and Churchill's attention with another emerging goal: containing the Communists. By early 1945, Germany was falling apart, and so were relations between former allies, namely the United States and the Soviet Union. On April 25 of that year, U.S. and Soviet troops met up at the Elbe River, just south of Berlin. The two armies danced, drank, and rejoiced together, and they did so again two weeks later, on May 7, when Germany finally surrendered. But by the end of the year, the United States and the Soviet Union would be openly hostile to one another, settling into a brand-new kind of conflict, one which would last more than forty years: a "cold war."

U.S. and Russian soldiers shake hands at the River Elbe, April 25, 1945

DEATH OF A TITAN

By the spring of 1945, Franklin Delano Roosevelt was sixty-three years old and had been president for twelve years, longer by half than any other chief executive in

U.S. history. He had led the country through the greatest
economic crisis the nation had ever seen and the greatest war the world had ever seen and now he was planning the greatest peace the world had ever seen. But it
had taken a toll on the man. While his wit and charm
were as apparent as ever, the president looked tired and
haggard and limited his public appearances. In February
1945, he attended a conference with Churchill and Stalin
at Yalta, in the Crimea region of the Soviet Union. The
three leaders discussed plans for postwar Europe and a
new international organization to settle disputes before
they developed into wars—the United Nations. Even so,
it was becoming more and more apparent that Stalin was
going to be as formidable an opponent as Hitler, perhaps more, and Roosevelt returned to the United States
drained of energy. When he addressed a joint session of
Congress after Yalta, he had to do so sitting down. "I
hope that you will pardon me for the unusual posture,"
he said. "It makes it a lot easier for me not having to
carry about ten pounds of steel around the bottom of
my legs." It was the only time he had ever referred to
his handicap in public.

Roosevelt soon retreated to Warm Springs, Georgia,
where he had built a vacation home some years earlier
in the futile hope that the local waters might cure his
polio. On the morning of April 12, 1945, after sitting for
a portrait, he complained of a headache; by afternoon,
he was dead. The cause was a cerebral hemorrhage. The
next day, Roosevelt's body was placed on a train and
sent north to Washington, D.C., for an official funeral;
he was eventually buried at his family estate in Hyde
Park, New York. Hundreds of thousands of people lined
the railroad tracks between Georgia and Washington to

LET'S GET TOGETHER AND TALK ABOUT IT

Hey, it's difficult to plan and run a war. FDR and the other Allied leaders often had to put their collective heads together to come up with a good plan. How often, you say?

1942:

The Rio Conference: Twenty-one North and South American nations pledged to sever relations with the Axis powers.

The Washington Conference: Roosevelt and Churchill planned the Allied invasion of North Africa.

The Moscow Conference: Churchill, Stalin, and U.S. diplomat W. Averell Harriman discussed joint strategy.

1943:

The Casablanca Conference: Roosevelt, Churchill, and other Allied representatives appointed General Eisenhower to command the North African campaign. They also decided on an invasion of Sicily and Italy, and a policy of unconditional surrender for the Axis powers.

The Trident Conference (Washington, D.C.): Roosevelt, Churchill, and their military advisers planned the D-Day invasion and troop displacements in Europe and the Pacific.

The Moscow Conference: Representatives from the United States, the United Kingdom, the Soviet Union, and China discussed plans for the postwar world and agreed to create an international organization for the pursuit of peace.

The Cairo Conference: Roosevelt, Churchill, and Chiang Kai-shek agreed that Japan must surrender unconditionally and return all the territory it had seized since World War I.

LET'S GET TOGETHER AND TALK ABOUT IT (*continued*)
....

The Teheran Conference: Roosevelt, Churchill, and Stalin agreed on the timing of the main European invasion.

1944:
The Dumbarton Oaks Conference (Washington, D.C.): Representatives from the United States, the United Kingdom, the Soviet Union, and China discussed further the formation of an international mechanism for peacefully resolving disputes in the postwar world.

The Octagon Conference (Quebec): Roosevelt and Churchill discussed strategies for defeating the Axis and the postwar world order.

1945:
The Yalta Conference: Roosevelt, Churchill, and Stalin discussed the final stage of the war in Europe and the postwar European order.

The Potsdam Conference: Truman, Churchill, and Stalin established the Council of Foreign Ministers from the United States, the United Kingdom, the Soviet Union, France, and China to work on international problems. The Potsdam Declaration called for Japan's unconditional surrender.

The San Francisco Conference: Representatives from different nations converged to work out and draw up the United Nations Charter.

pay their last respects; many of them, in tears, said they felt as if they'd lost a close friend.

Shortly after the president died, Mrs. Roosevelt summoned Vice President Harry S Truman to the White House and said, simply, "the President is dead." "Is there anything I can do for you?" Truman asked her. Mrs. Roosevelt replied: "Is there anything *we* can do for *you*? For you are the one in trouble now."

PRESIDENT WHO?

If Dwight D. Eisenhower had seemed like an unusual choice when he was tapped to lead the Allied forces in Europe, Harry S. Truman was all but unknown outside his home state of Missouri when FDR chose him for vice president in 1944. Actually, he was still pretty much unknown when he became president, less than a year later.

Harry S. Truman was a most unusual politician and president, but then again, he was a most unusual human being. For one thing, he didn't actually have a middle name; his parents couldn't agree on one, so they compromised by just giving him a middle initial, *S.* For another, he never attended college, his family's finances having taken a turn for the worst when he was a child. As a young man in Independence, Missouri, he had held a string of deadend jobs—mailroom clerk at a newspaper, bookkeeper for a bank, timekeeper for a railroad construction crew—and was still living at home with his parents at the age of thirty-three. Then America entered World War I, and Truman joined the army. He was popular among his fellow soldiers, who elected him captain of their unit—Battery D of the 129th Field Artillery. The company was soon shipped to France and participated in some of the heaviest fighting of 1918. By all accounts, Truman was an exceptionally brave soldier who often put himself in very dangerous positions.

He returned to Independence a hero, married his

childhood sweetheart, Bess Wallace (he was thirty-five, she thirty-four) and went into business for himself, opening a haberdashery in Kansas City. But within two years the business had failed, and Truman, desperate to avoid bankruptcy, turned to politics. A war buddy was the nephew of Tom Pendergast, Kansas City's political boss, and the machine sponsored Truman for the position of judge for the eastern district of Jackson County, Missouri (the position was strictly administrative, and had nothing to do with trying cases or ruling on questions of law). Truman soon earned a reputation for honesty and incorruptibility, and he became extremely popular by cutting government waste, thereby saving taxpayers a lot of money. In 1934, he was elected to the U.S. Senate, where he had a fairly undistinguished first term.

In 1940, when Truman came up for re-election to the Senate, President Roosevelt actually favored Truman's opponent in the Democratic primary, and tried to get Truman to drop out of the race by offering him a seat on the Interstate Commerce Commission. Truman declined and, hampered further by a tiny budget, actually drove himself all over Missouri to campaign. He narrowly won re-election, and returned to the Senate with a new zeal for his reform and, especially, for cutting waste in defense spending. The Senate, anxious to pacify Truman, appointed him to head an investigatory committee, thinking he would fade into the woodwork. But then the war came, and Truman's committee was suddenly thrust into the spotlight. By 1944, he had saved taxpayers many billions of dollars, and his contribution to the war effort was deemed so important that Roosevelt personally drafted him to join his ticket as vice president.

Now, just four months after being elected vice president, Harry S. Truman found himself in the White House. Nothing he had done since his inauguration had prepared him for the job that was now his; indeed, he and Roosevelt had met only a few times in the months before FDR's death. Fortunately, the war with Germany was wrapping up, but there was still Japan to worry about; just that month, the U.S. Army had started its battle to take the island of Okinawa, a fight that would eventually claim 80,000 U.S. casualties and 120,000 Japanese. As the Allies drew closer and closer to Japan itself, they met fiercer and fiercer resistance from increasingly desperate Japanese troops. Many now believed that nothing short of an all-out invasion of Japan would bring about that country's surrender, and that such an invasion would cost a million American lives.

Then Truman learned about America's secret weapon.

YES, IT REALLY WAS A SECRET WEAPON

In 1939, President Roosevelt was informed that German scientists had successfully accomplished atomic fission in uranium. That summer, the physicist Albert Einstein stated in a letter to FDR that two scientists working in America, Enrico Fermi and Leo Szilard, had been doing their own experiments with uranium. Einstein asked the president to establish a government-funded program to investigate the possibility of using atomic fission as a source of energy. Three years later, with the war in progress, Roosevelt, worried that the Germans might develop an atomic bomb, created the Manhattan District, a section of the Army Corps of Engineers. The Manhattan

District had one objective: to create a nuclear chain reaction, and, ultimately, an atomic bomb. This project, which would take almost three years, would be known, not surprisingly, as the Manhattan Project.

Albert Einstein

On December 2, 1942, the team of scientists, which included Fermi, Szilard, and Edward Teller, created a controlled, self-sustaining nuclear chain reaction in uranium at the University of Chicago (melting concrete in the process). The Manhattan Project now focused entirely on creating an atomic bomb; in 1943, the team, under the leadership of thirty-nine-year-old physicist J. Robert Oppenheimer and the army's General Leslie R. Groves, moved to a government laboratory in Los Alamos, New Mexico. Plants in Oak Ridge, Tennessee and Hanford, Washington were used to produce the materials necessary to make the bomb. It was a massive project, involving 125,000 people at a cost of $2 billion.

Finally, on July 16, 1945, the first atomic test explosion took place in the desert at Alamogordo, New Mexico.

The atomic bomb was now a reality. The only question was how, and where, it would be used. Many of the scientists who had helped make the bomb a reality regretted their efforts even before the project had been completed.

That decision fell to the new president. Truman had to consider the damage the bomb would cause, the innocent lives it would take. He also had to consider the potential casualties incurred in a U.S. invasion of Japan. Truman must have known that generations yet unborn would debate the merits of his decision, whatever he chose. Ultimately, he decided to use the weapon against Japan, in the hope that it would convince that nation to surrender before an invasion would be launched. On August 6, 1945, a U.S. B-29 bomber, the *Enola Gay,* dropped the first atomic bomb, "Little Boy" on the industrial city of Hiroshima, Japan; three days later, a second bomb, "Fat Man," was dropped on the city of Nagasaki. Both cities were largely destroyed; 200,000 Japanese men, women, and children had been killed by the bombs. On August 14, Japan surrendered.

The war was over.

WELL, SO MUCH FOR THE DEPRESSION

Now, no doubt about it, war is a bad thing, even for the winners. The United States lost nearly 300,000 soldiers, sailors, and marines in World War II, and many of the fighting men who survived the war were faced with the grisly tasks of liberating Nazi concentration camps

The first atomic bomb exploding over Hiroshima, Japan

(where some 14 million people—among them Poles, Slavs, Gypsies, homosexuals, political prisoners, and Jews—had been murdered), disposing of thousands of burned and emaciated bodies, guarding hundreds of thousands of homeless refugees in "displaced persons" camps, and clearing away the rubble of devastated cities. It was a messy, awful job.

Even so, it could be said that, in 1945, America sat on top of the world. When the shooting stopped, the United States was the most powerful nation on earth, the most powerful in history. In fact, no one else even came close. Our soldiers were stationed all over Europe and Asia. We had nuclear supremacy. We helped Germany and Japan rebuild themselves and establish democratic governments. And the Depression? Well, that was just a distant, if bitter, memory. Hard times were over—way over. Everyone, it seemed, had a job. And not just a job but a job that paid well. GI loans helped returning soldiers buy their first homes; the GI Bill helped them get college degrees. In fact, it is scarcely an exaggeration to say that, in 1945, the United States had almost all the money on the planet.

Of course, that kind of prosperity—in a world that was still, for the most part, devastated—came with a price. The price was a hefty responsibility to see to it that World War III never happened, that people were able to vote and determine their own forms of government, that hunger and homelessness became things of the past, that Communism be kept from spreading across the planet, undermining everything that the United States had gone to war for in the first place. It wouldn't be easy; some of it would never be accomplished. But the post–World War II United States was an extremely idealistic country, a nation with a notion that it could accomplish almost anything. In the years and decades to come, of course, that notion would be disproved time and time again.

On the other hand, a lot did come out of that ideal-

SAY, THIS RADIO LOOKS A LITTLE FUNNY

At the New York World's Fair in 1939, RCA (the Radio Corporation of America) unveiled a new kind of radio set. This one featured moving pictures as well as sound.

Television had been in the works since the 1920s, and ever since, RCA, the world's leading radio manufacturer, had led the field in trying to develop this new medium, pouring millions of dollars and manpower hours into the quest—never worrying, apparently, that it might just make their current bread-and-butter obsolete (it never did, of course, but still . . .). By 1939, RCA was ready to introduce television to the world, which it did at its special World's Fair pavilion, which was shaped like a vacuum tube.

RCA and other manufacturers did sell quite a few rudimentary TV sets to the general public in 1939 and 1940 (although "general" might not be a fair term; the new invention was *very* expensive to purchase), but then, like almost everything else, television development and production was interrupted by the war. The government needed RCA to focus its attentions on manufacturing communications equipment for the armed forces, and RCA was eager to oblige.

In 1946, with the war over, production of TV sets geared up once again. Initial sales, though, were sluggish, despite the fact that prices were dramatically lower than they had been before the war. The problem, simply, was that there just wasn't anything on, at least nothing worth watching. Radio, with its long-beloved serials and shows, remained the dominant medium.

By the end of the decade, though, television was starting to supersede radio, and this radical turnabout can be attributed to one man: Milton Berle. In 1948, Berle, a former vaudeville star, debuted his own variety show, sponsored by Texaco, on Tuesday nights. There was nothing else like it on television, and it quickly

---

SAY, THIS RADIO LOOKS A LITTLE FUNNY
(*continued*)
. . . .
became a massive hit. Berle is credited with selling
more TV sets than any other individual or company in
America, and the boom was quite dramatic; the number
of U.S. households with a TV set soared from 949,000
in 1949 to 20 million in 1953.

---

ism, like the Nuremberg war crimes trials (in which
judges from the Allied nations determined the account-
ability of the chief German architects of the war, the
Holocaust, and other Nazi atrocities, sentencing twelve
of them to death), the United Nations (which continues
to play an important role in international relations to
this day), the North Atlantic Treaty Organization (which
does, too), and a recovery program that made FDR's
New Deal look like a pittance in comparison.

SOUNDS LIKE A PLAN TO ME

Unlike most generals, George C. Marshall was as concerned with winning the peace as he had been with winning the war. He retired from service in the fall of 1945,
but was almost immediately sent to China on an unsuccessful mission to negotiate a peace between the Nationalist government and Mao Tse-tung's Communist forces.
In January 1947, President Truman named Marshall as
his new Secretary of State.

   While attending conferences in Europe that spring, it
became apparent to Marshall that most of the Continent
was teetering on the brink of economic collapse; even

worse, Marshall observed, the Soviet Union was preparing to capitalize on the crisis that would surely ensue. The Soviets had already occupied East Germany, Poland, Czechoslovakia, Romania, and Hungary during the turmoil at the end of the war; Marshall was determined to keep them from encroaching any further into central Europe. The best defense, he reasoned, was to make the "western bloc" strong enough to stand on its own. On June 5, 1947, he unveiled his plan during a commencement address at Harvard.

"The Marshall plan," as Truman named it, called for the United States to funnel funds into central and western Europe; the goal was, literally, to rebuild the Continent, enabling the individual nations to embark on the road to economic recovery, and, ultimately, to restore "the confidence of the European people in the economic future of their own countries and of Europe as a whole." It worked. From 1948 to 1951, the United States gave these nations more than $13 billion in aid—without, not surprisingly, the help of the Soviet Union, which vehemently opposed the plan as heavy-handed American interventionism. Those countries that participated in the program soon became strong enough to build stable economies on their own; those that didn't—like Poland and Czechoslovakia, prevented by the Soviets from accepting U.S. aid—faltered and remained dependent upon the Soviet Union.

The Marshall plan was, perhaps, the largest foreign policy initiative in U.S. history. On one level, it was a stunning success; but it also served to deepen the rift between the United States and the Soviet Union, the world's two indisputable superpowers. And the cold war got colder and colder.

Now, when you're the only nuclear power in the world, you can throw your weight around a little. In March 1947, the president unveiled the Truman doctrine, which called for the United States to spend up to $400 million to protect ostensibly "democratic" countries from capitulating to the Communist threat. In other words, Truman was playing hardball with the Soviets. He had already gotten them to withdraw their troops from northern Persia by threatening an atomic attack. The story goes that Truman said something like this to Stalin: "We have the bomb. You don't. If you're not out of there in forty-eight hours, we'll drop it on you." Whether or not Truman actually used those exact words, it worked; the Soviets were out in twenty-four hours.

A year later, Truman successfully used a more conventional "weapon"—money—to help Greece and Turkey defeat Communist insurrections. He also started sending massive amounts of aid to the Allied zones of Germany (following a policy that became known as the Truman Doctrine). Stalin felt threatened by the prospect of a strong and democratic West Germany, and was especially incensed at the persistent Allied military presence in West Berlin (the city of Berlin, deep inside Communist East Germany, had been divided after the war into two halves, one "free," the other Communist). In an attempt to quash this, the Soviets "blockaded" Berlin, preventing any Western access to the city and threatening to starve the Western presence out of the city. Truman was determined to get supplies to the besieged city, and he did so the only way he could—by airplane. The "Berlin airlift" lasted 321 days; in that time, Western pilots made more than 270,000 flights into the city, delivering millions of tons of crucial supplies. By May 1949, realizing

The children of Berlin cheer U.S. planes

that they had lost both the battle and public sympathy, the Soviets abandoned their blockade.

It would be one of the last clear-cut victories for the United States in the cold war, at least for another four decades. On September 23, 1949, President Truman made a grim announcement to the American public: The Soviet Union had successfully detonated its own atomic bomb. The era of unchallenged American supremacy in the world was over.

AN INCUMBENT UNDERDOG

Harry Truman was always up for a good fight. In 1948, he got one. But it wasn't in Germany or Poland or Korea; it was right here, at home. And his enemy wasn't the Soviet Union; it was the Republican Party.

In November 1946, the Republicans, playing on a re-worked version of Warren G. Harding's "Return to Normalcy," ("Had Enough?" was a popular GOP slogan that year) recaptured both houses of Congress for the first time since Herbert Hoover was president. For the next two years, Congress fought Truman on virtually every single piece of domestic legislation the president favored. The Democrats weren't much better; within the party itself, Truman faced challenges on both the right and the left, and one Democratic senator, J. William Fulbright of Arkansas, actually tried to get Truman to resign. Henry Wallace, FDR's vice president from 1940 to 1944, ran for president on the Progressive ticket and took 5 million votes from Truman. Southern Democrats, condemning Truman as soft on the race issue, defected, as well; the "Dixiecrats," as they became known, backed South Carolina Senator Strom Thurmond for president. And it was only after failing to convince Eisenhower to run for president in 1948 that the remaining Democrats resigned themselves to backing Truman for a second term. At the convention, Truman gave a rousing speech to an apathetic audience; some commented that Truman was the only man in the country who believed he could win the election.

Instead of running against his well-financed opponent, Thomas E. Dewey, the governor of New York—a genuinely decent and honest man who had run against FDR in 1944—Truman campaigned against what he called the "do-nothing Republican Congress." He barnstormed the country, appearing in big cities and small towns alike, trying to arouse ire against cold-hearted "Republican gluttons of privilege" who "want a return of the Wall Street dictatorship," the kind of arrangement that would leave farmers and small businessmen out in the cold. Occasionally, someone in the audience would get fired up at Truman's impassioned oratory and shout, "Give 'em hell, Harry!" But Truman's campaign was in trouble. He was so short of funds that radio stations occasionally silenced his microphone in the middle of a speech after discovering that Truman couldn't pay for the airtime.

On Election Day, November 2, 1948, Dewey was heavily favored, and even though early returns showed Truman in the lead, the *Chicago Daily Tribune,* racing to make an early deadline, printed up the headline, "DEWEY DEFEATS TRUMAN." The next morning, when the results were all in, it wasn't even that close; Truman had won by a margin of 2.2 million popular votes and 114 electoral votes. Truman posed for a now-famous photograph, holding aloft the erroneous newspaper headline proclaiming his defeat, his face lit up by a broad, toothy smile.

Strom Thurmond, the Dixiecrat candidate from South Carolina, had drawn thrity-nine electoral votes, all of them in the South. Southern Democrats had deserted their party's candidate in July, after Truman had issued an executive order immediately ending racial segregation in every branch of the armed forces as well as in federal employment. Just a year earlier, Jackie Robinson, the first African-American to play in major league baseball in the twentieth century, had made his debut with the Brooklyn Dodgers. These two events—and a war that would break out halfway across the world on June 25, 1950—would set the stage to define the United States in the decades to come.

CHAPTER 7

THE REST OF THE STORY

U.S. POPULATION:
150,697,361 (1950)
179,323,175 (1960)
203,211,926 (1970)
226,504,825 (1980)
249,632,692 (1990)

UH, BEFORE YOU HANG UP THAT UNIFORM . . .

It is commonly assumed that since 1945, the United States has been a nation, for the most part, at peace. Of course, the thing about common assumptions is that they're commonly wrong.

True, America has not gotten itself involved in another global war in the past half century. It is also true that the United States has done more than any other nation in the world to prevent such a global conflict from ever happening again. But the United States has become embroiled in two major wars since the close of World War II, wars that dragged on for decades, claimed untold American lives, and generally disrupted business as usual, so much so that "business as usual," as a concept, barely even exists anymore.

The thing is, both of these wars—which raged concurrently—were undeclared, unofficial wars. One was a good old-fashioned foreign war; the other was a civil war, fought on American streets and in American parks, in small American towns and large American cities. To the former, we have assigned a formal name: the Cold War. The latter could very well be called the Cold Civil War, but it is better known, today, as the Civil Rights Movement.

PART I: THE COLD WAR

BRRRRR . . . IS THERE A DRAFT IN HERE?

The Cold War, as we've seen, was a direct result of the hottest war in history—namely, World War II. It was also a bit of a misnomer, because it did, at times, get quite hot. And the increasing proliferation of nuclear weapons meant that, for the very first time, the threat of a "hot" war also carried with it the possibility that things might get so hot that planet earth could no longer support life. Given such devastating potential, even the "smallest" military conflicts assumed the importance—and tension—of a global war. The stakes were unimaginably high; keeping the peace between the two superpowers,

Triumph of Communist Mao Zedong, Mailand China, 1949

the United States and the Soviet Union, became a very delicate balancing act.

For the first five years after the end of World War II, that delicate balance between peace and war held fairly steady, despite challenges in Persia and Turkey, Greece and Berlin. On the other side of the world, though, trouble was brewing. In 1949, Mao Tse-tung's Communist insurgents drove Chiang Kai-shek's Nationalist government into exile on the island of Formosa, which they soon renamed Taiwan; Mao renamed his nation the People's Republic of China, and soon signed a treaty with Soviet dictator Joseph Stalin.

Almost immediately after China fell, tension began building in neighboring Korea, a small peninsular nation adjacent to China, which had been occupied by Japan during the War. In the fall of 1945, just days before the Japanese surrender, the Soviet Union had declared war on Japan; when the war ended, the United States and the Soviet Union agreed to split Korea laterally along the 38th parallel, with the Soviet Union occupying the northern half, America the southern. Consequently, the Soviets helped establish a communist government in North Korea, while the United States promoted democracy in South Korea. Almost immediately, tensions developed between the two halves, a situation that was exacerbated by the growing tensions between the two superpowers.

On June 25, 1950—with the knowledge and approval of Stalin and armed with Soviet weapons—North Korean armies crossed the border and invaded South Korea.

General Douglas MacArthur in Asia

They quickly overran ill-prepared South Korean troops and pushed deep into enemy territory, capturing most of South Korea, including the capital, Seoul. The United Nations Security Council, spurred on by the United States, issued a formal condemnation of the invasion, and established a fighting force, the U.N. Command, to restore the peace. President Truman immediately committed U.S. troops to the effort, and General Douglas MacArthur, the hero of the Pacific war, was assigned to head the new force. Fifteen other U.N. member nations also committed troops to the fight.

On September 15, MacArthur led his forces in a bold and successful amphibious landing at Inchon; eleven days later, they recaptured Seoul from the communists; by the twenty-ninth, they had pushed the North Koreans back across the 38th parallel. On October 7, U.N. forces crossed the line and invaded North Korea. China condemned the invasion and warned that it would take action if the United Nations did not withdraw immediately; ignoring China's threat, MacArthur pushed ahead. By November 20, U.N. soldiers had reached the Yalu River, the border between North Korea and Manchuria, China.

Six days later, Chinese soldiers flooded over the border, stunning the U.N. forces; within weeks, they had been pushed back over the 38th parallel again. MacArthur, frustrated, called for an attack on China itself, including a naval blockade, aerial bombardment, and an invasion. Truman, regarding MacArthur as both insubordinate and a megalomaniac and worried that an attack on China might start a new world war, fired the general and replaced him with General Matthew Ridgway, who had commanded the Eighty-second Airborne during World War II. Truman was widely criticized for the action, MacArthur received a hero's welcome back at home, and the war quickly became a bloody stalemate.

After two years of peace negotiations, the two Koreas signed an armistice on July 27, 1953; the border remained close to where it had been before the war had begun. Neither side was pleased with the peace and hostility remained. As for the United States, the price it paid for this conflict was more than 50,000 U.S. soldiers killed, another 8,000 or so missing, and 100,000 more injured—a high casualty rate for a war that wasn't, technically, "hot."

THE MORE THINGS CHANGE . . .

On March 5, 1953, Soviet leader Josef Stalin died at the age of 73. Apart from everything else that has been said about him—namely, that he was ruthless, paranoid, bloodthirsty, megalomaniacal, tyrannical, and personally responsible for the deaths of tens of millions of his "countrymen"—for most Americans, Stalin had quickly come to symbolize the enemy in the Cold War. Stalin had ruled the Soviet Union as a virtual dictator for nearly thirty years; his death left most people wondering how his removal from the scene might change the scene itself.

The early answer: not much. Stalin's post as chairman of the Council of Ministers was filled by Soviet war hero Georgy Malenkov. The position of Communist Party Secretary was filled by a fifty-eight-year-old party functionary named Nikita Khruschev. It would be Khruschev who would eventually come to stand as a symbol for the Soviet Union during the height—or depths—of the Cold War.

Meanwhile, President Truman, who had chosen not to run for another term, had been replaced on the Democratic ticket by Governor Adlai Ewing Stevenson III of Illinois. The Republicans drafted General Dwight D. Eisenhower as their presidential candidate. Eisenhower was a war hero, head of NATO, and president of Columbia University; Stevenson, a fairly low-key and intellectual man, was quickly labeled, by his opponents, everything from an egghead to effeminate.

Eisenhower's campaign, however, suffered a setback when a bit of a scandal broke concerning questionable campaign contributions to his running mate, a thirty-nine-year-old first-term California senator named Richard Milhous Nixon. Specifically, Nixon was accused of building a cache of $18,235, mostly with donations from California Republicans. As Eisenhower considered dropping Nixon from the ticket, Nixon went on national television—at a cost of $75,000, more than four times the size of the campaign fund—and denied having done anything wrong. He had accepted contributions, he admitted, but only to fight Communism, and none of the money had gone directly to him, anyway. Then he did specify one gift he had accepted: "A little cocker spaniel dog in a crate that was sent all the way from Texas. Black and white spotted. And our little girl—Tricia, the six-year-old—named it Checkers. And you know, the kids love the dog, and I just want to say this right now, that regardless of what they say about it, we're gonna keep it!" He was near tears. The public ate it up.

Nixon stayed on the ticket. Eisenhower won the election in what can fairly be termed a landslide. Four years later, he and Stevenson would go at it again, with similar results.

Eisenhower quickly made good on his most memorable campaign promise: "I will go to Korea." Not much of a promise, but he did go in December 1952, and

President Eisenhower

seven months into Eisenhower's first year, the war in Korea was over. The United States, it would seem, had won a major battle of the Cold War. But just two weeks later, on August 12, 1953, the Soviet Union detonated the first hydrogen bomb, giving them an edge, for the time being, in the arms race.

And things just kept getting hotter. And colder.

COLD WAR, HOT AIR

When China, the world's most populous nation, fell to Mao Tse-tung and his Communists in 1949, a panic swept across the West, and especially the United States. Throughout the country, people in public and private wondered aloud who was responsible for "losing" China. Some people did more than just wonder; they started blaming people. Among the targets were President Truman, the U.S. Army, Congress, the CIA, and the usual suspects: leftists. In 1919, the leftists had been deported as "reds"; in the 1920s and 1930s, they were ostracized as "troublemakers" and "rabble-rousers." Now they were about to be hunted as "pink" or "Communist sympathizers."

One of the key instruments in this hunt was a congressional organization, the House Un-American Activities Committee (HUAC), which had been formed originally in 1938 to investigate fascists and Nazi sympathizers in America. In the late 1940s, HUAC turned its attention to rooting out Communists and Communist sympathizers in government, but soon expanded its investigations into the arts and entertainment—most notably into Hollywood, which, some suspected, was teeming with Communists who conspired to use the movies to spread their dogma across middle America. While HUAC never did uncover a Communist conspiracy in Hollywood, dozens of writers, directors, and actors were "blacklisted," labeled "pink" by the committee and unable to secure work at studios or television networks that, afraid of being tarnished by association, refused to hire them. Some, especially writers, were able to get jobs using aliases, and some were able to return to the industry after a decade or more, but many others never worked again.

Even the powerful HUAC, though, was upstaged by a lone man. In February 1950, Joseph McCarthy, a little-known first-term senator from Wisconsin, was giving a speech to a Republican women's club in Wheeling, West Virginia, when he held up a piece of paper and announced that it contained a list of 205 Communists working for the State Department. Two weeks later, McCarthy claimed he had compiled another such list, prompting the Senate to form a special subcommittee to investigate. Never mind that McCarthy never actually *showed* either list to anyone or that his numbers varied from day to day or that he refused, when questioned, to present further proof. Many Americans, still reeling from the news that the Soviets had the atomic bomb and China had been "lost," were in a state of near-panic about the "red menace" and were inclined to believe that Communists were just about everywhere. McCarthy became famous overnight, personifying the anti-Communist hysteria that was sweeping the nation, a panic that he had played a large part in generating.

The Senate subcommittee hearings never found much substance to McCarthy's charges. Still, McCarthy continued to make headlines and win the support of Republi-

Senator Joseph McCarthy speaking to the special Senate subcommittee

can Party leaders, mostly because he targeted President Truman's Democratic administration. But even after Republican Dwight D. Eisenhower was elected president in 1952, McCarthy refused to let up; instead, he started attacking new targets, including the Army Signal Corps, the Voice of America radio network, and World War II hero General George C. Marshall, President Eisenhower's mentor. But in 1954, McCarthy accused the U.S. Army itself of promoting Communism. The charges— and the army's countercharges that McCarthy had requested preferential treatment for an aide who had been drafted—led to a new set of hearings that were broadcast live on television. McCarthy came across as a liar, a bully, and a buffoon, and the Senate voted to censure him. The age of McCarthyism had come to an end. Three years later, he was dead.

THE FINAL FRONTIER (WITH APOLOGIES TO GENE RODDENBERRY)

Since the dawn of civilization, men and women have looked skyward and wondered, "Hey! What's really up there, anyway? And how can I check it out?" In the 1950s, President Eisenhower decided that it was time mankind answered those questions once and for all, and that Americans lead the way. Not surprisingly, the Soviets had the same idea, only they were determined to lead the way. That, in one sense, was what the Cold War was all about: keeping up with the Joneses. Except that, in this case, the Joneses were on the other side of the world, held sway over huge chunks of the planet, and possessed the power and the means to destroy the earth, if they so desired. Not exactly "my lawn is greener than yours" or "guess who just got a brand-new color television set?" but not really all that different, either.

Anyway, throughout the mid-1950s, both the United States and the Soviet Union had teams of brilliant scientists working tirelessly on building a rocket that would carry man-made objects—and even man himself—to the moon, the stars, and beyond. This quickly became known as "the space race," and while some people considered it a matter of national security, believing that whoever reached outer space first would control it and thus possess an inestimable military and defense advantage—sort of like the high ground in a battle, only much, much higher—others saw the whole thing as a competition for bragging rights.

In any event, the United States lost this particular race. On October 4, 1957, the Soviets launched Sputnik I, the world's first man-made satellite, into orbit; it would circle the globe every ninety minutes. Never mind that Sputnik was roughly the size and shape of a basketball, weighed a mere 184 pounds, and had a ludicrous name, besides; contest over, bragging rights awarded to the Soviet Union. A month later, the Soviets launched Sputnik II, which weighed more than a thousand pounds and contained, among other things, the first live space traveler, a dog named Laika. The *New York Times* would report overhearing Russian citizens grumbling "better to learn to feed your people at home before starting to explore the moon," but for many Americans that news would come as cold comfort. So would the announcement, the following January, that the United States was launching its own satellite, Explorer I.

On October 1, 1958, the National Aeronautics and Space Administration (NASA) was created. NASA would

replace the National Advisory Committee for Aeronautics (NACA), an agency that had been around since 1915, when Orville Wright was still puttering with his flying machines. NACA had helped develop aviation technology; NASA was charged with the mission of sending satellites and, eventually, civilians into space, a mission that soon became known as the space program. Its first mandate was to make the United States the first country to send a man into space.

Alas, we lost that race, too. On April 12, 1961, the Soviet Union launched cosmonaut Yuri Gagarin into space; Gagarin orbited the earth once and returned safely. Three weeks later, NASA sent its first astronaut, Alan Sheppard, into space for a fifteen-minute suborbital flight. (What's the difference between an astronaut and a cosmonaut? Good question.) The following February, John Glenn became the first American to orbit the earth.

Glenn returned to earth a hero; the success of his mission would be more than enough to make most Americans forget that he had not been first. Not until 1969 would the United States assume unquestioned supremacy in the space race by becoming the first nation to put a man—astronaut Neil Armstrong—on the moon. The sight of the Stars and Stripes planted in the lunar surface was, for many Americans, proof that the United States would ultimately prevail in the Cold War.

MEANWHILE, BACK ON EARTH

In 1959, though, the Cold War was far from over—or, for that matter, won. On January 1 of that year, Fidel Castro, the thirty-two-year-old leader of a two-year insurrection in Cuba, managed to drive dictator Fulgencio Batista right off the island. (Batista eventually ended up in Miami, along with many thousands of Cuban refugees.) Castro, who had once tried out for the Washington Senators baseball team, visited the United States that April, declaring himself a "humanist," not a Communist. At first, Castro was warmly regarded by much of this country as a human alternative to the despotic Batista. But Castro soon made it apparent that he was not altogether unfamiliar with, or unsympathetic to, Marxism. As Castro began walking and talking more and more like a Communist, and accepting more and more aid from the Soviet Union—especially in the form of arms—many people in the United States began to regard the bearded, cigar-chomping man in army fatigues with fear and loathing. After all, as anyone could have told you, Cuba was only ninety miles away from Florida. Eisenhower declared that the United States would not tolerate a Communist regime in the Western Hemisphere; Khruschev declared that he would use Soviet rockets to protect Cuba, if necessary. All in all, a messy situation.

Fidel Castro

As if that wasn't bad enough, on May 1, 1960, the Soviets shot down a top-secret U.S. U-2 spy plane that had been flying some 60,000 feet over Siberia. The U-2, which the United States had officially stated didn't exist, had been making reconnaissance flights over the Soviet Union, something the United States had officially denied doing. The plane, which was supposed to self-destruct upon impact, didn't; the pilot, who was supposed to commit suicide rather than be captured, didn't, either. The pilot, thirty-year-old Francis Gary Powers, was quickly captured by Soviet authorities, forcing Eisenhower to acknowledge that the United States really had been running spy flights over the Soviet Union, after all.

Khruschev used the incident as an excuse to cancel a planned peace summit with Eisenhower in Paris. As Eisenhower's term ran out at the end of 1960, U.S.–Soviet relations hit what was arguably their lowest point ever. Not really the best way for the new president—a forty-three-year-old senator from Massachusetts named John Fitzgerald Kennedy—to take office.

THIS, I NEED?

John F. Kennedy was elected president on November 8, 1960, defeating incumbent Vice President Richard M. Nixon in the closest presidential election in U.S. history. In fact, the margin was so close—Kennedy received just 113,057 more popular votes than Nixon, out of a total of some 69 million—that many people believed (and still believe) that Kennedy, the scion of an extremely rich, powerful and well-connected family, only managed to secure victory by somewhat less-than-honest means. If true, Kennedy might very well have wondered, as he assumed the highest office in the United States, if it was worth the trouble.

Trouble, it seemed, was what the office offered from the very start. Even before the election, the Central Intelligence Agency had begun training an army of some two thousand Cuban exiles in Central America, planning an invasion of their home island, with naval and air support from the United States, that would start an insurrection and eventually lead to Castro's downfall—or so the plan went. By the time Kennedy became president and learned of the plan, training was already near completion. Kennedy approved the invasion. On April 17, 1961,

President John F. Kennedy

the secret army stormed the shores of Cuba at the Bay of Pigs, but the air and sea support they expected never came, and they were quickly captured by Cuban troops. The U.S. State Department at first denied any involvement. A few days later, though, Kennedy declared that the invasion was a mistake and claimed full responsibility. The United States appeared to have been defeated by a tiny Caribbean island; Cuba, the Soviet Union, and Soviet bloc nations heaped scorn upon the United States and John F. Kennedy.

The following year, U.S. aerial reconnaissance discovered that Soviet bomber and missile bases were being built in Cuba. On October 22, 1962, Kennedy made this information public, along with a demand that the Soviet Union dismantle the bases and remove the weapons immediately. Fearful that Soviet ships were already en route to the island, he also dispatched U.S. ships to blockade

Cuba. For several days, as Soviet ships continued on their course toward Cuba and U.S. ships held their positions, millions of Americans and Soviets worried that the war they had dreaded for nearly two decades—the war that could literally mean the end of the world—was, at last, about to begin. Finally, on October 28, Kennedy and Khruschev struck a deal: Khruschev would remove Soviet missiles from Cuba in exchange for a promise that the United States would not attack the island. The crisis was over; in the most tense conflict of the Cold War, the United States had emerged victorious. Two years later, Khruschev would be removed from office, having lost favor for his "lenience" toward the West.

By then, though, Kennedy would be dead. On November 22, 1963, Kennedy, riding a wave of great popularity, traveled to Dallas, Texas, on an early campaign trip for the 1964 election. As his open limousine rode through the streets, Kennedy was shot twice by a sniper and died almost immediately. Lee Harvey Oswald, a twenty-four-year-old former U.S. Marine who had lived in the Soviet Union and had taken a Russian wife, was arrested later that day and charged with the shooting; many suspected that Oswald had ties to Cuba, too. Just a few days later, however, while being moved to another jail, Oswald was himself fatally shot by Jack Ruby, a Dallas nightclub owner who claimed that he wanted to spare Mrs. Kennedy the trauma of a trial. This bizarre series of events—as well as Oswald's insistence before he was killed that he was just a "patsy"—have led some to state that Oswald was only one player in a vast conspiracy, or perhaps not involved at all, and that Kennedy was assassinated at the behest of Castro, the CIA, the Mafia, or any number of other shadowy figures or organizations.

THIS, I NEED?: PART II

Whatever the case, Kennedy was dead, and Vice President Lyndon Baines Johnson, a former Texas Senator, inherited a mess at least as great as the one his predecessor had found in 1961. For years—specifically, since 1954, when the French were driven out of a colony of theirs by a native Communist army—the United States had been sending "military advisers" to the country that the French had called Indochina and the locals called Vietnam. It had been split, after World War II, very much as Korea had been: down the middle, with Communists up north and Democrats down south (although, to be accurate, the Communists up north were more Marxist than Communist, and the Democrats down south were hardly democratic, but that's a whole book in and of itself). Eisenhower continued to send more troops, money, and arms to South Vietnam, justifying it by what he called the "domino theory": If Vietnam fell to the Communists, Communism would quickly spread to the rest of Southeast Asia, then the rest of Asia (hey, it already had China), then the rest of the world. Kennedy picked up where Eisenhower left off, ultimately tripling the amount of U.S. aid to that country; by 1963, when Kennedy was assassinated, there were some 16,000 U.S. military advisers in South Vietnam.

This left Johnson in a quandary: If he continued sending men and money to Vietnam, a war seemed imminent; but if he pulled the men out and ended the support, he risked "losing" Vietnam just as China had been "lost" in 1949. Johnson, a brilliant politician who always seemed acutely aware of and concerned about how history would remember him, decided to risk war,

Lyndon B. Johnson

instead. In the first week of August 1964, two U.S. destroyers were fired upon while sailing through the Gulf of Tonkin off North Vietnam, they returned fire, and sank two North Vietnamese boats. Johnson quickly got Congress to pass the Gulf of Tonkin Resolution, granting him the power to "take all necessary measures to repel any armed attack against the forces of the United States and to prevent further aggression." The resolution, in effect, granted power to declare war without actually declaring war, which requires congressional approval.

That fall, Johnson ran for president against Republican Barry Goldwater of Arizona, who was portrayed as irresponsibly extremist and aggressive; Johnson won in a landslide, then proceeded to send massive numbers of combat troops to Vietnam—more than 300,000 by the following summer. Still, Johnson, ever mindful of his place in history, did not want to become the first U.S. president to lose a war; instead, he decided to hold back and keep the conflict somewhat "limited," to stifle it from growing into an all-out war by not pursuing victory with every means at his disposal— by not using nuclear weapons, for instance. He chose to defeat the enemy by waging a war of attrition. He had the air force drop conventional bombs on North Vietnam, and lots of them—so many, that by 1967, the United States had dropped more tonnage on North Vietnam than the Allies had on Germany, Japan, and Italy in all of World War II. And by the following year, there were a half million U.S. troops in Vietnam.

Late in 1967, the United States believed that this strategy of attrition was working. But in January 1968, the North Vietnamese and their guerrilla army, the Vietcong, launched a surprise offensive that coincided with Tet, the Vietnamese new year celebration, even managing to penetrate the U.S. embassy compound in Saigon, the capital of South Vietnam. Militarily, the move was ultimately a failure; U.S. and South Vietnamese troops repulsed the Vietcong on all fronts and inflicted heavy casualties. But the Tet Offensive, as it soon became known, was a huge public relations victory for North Vietnam. It now appeared that the war of attrition was clearly not working, that the Vietcong could go wherever they wished, and that the United States would never be able to fully defeat them short of declaring and prosecuting a full-scale war. In the states, where it had always been controversial, the war soon became downright unpopular among both the left, which objected to any American presence in the area, and the right, which objected to sending U.S. troops to fight without the full-fledged support of the U.S. military and government. Massive protests erupted across the country; Democrats, starting with Senator Eugene McCarthy of Minnesota, began challenging Johnson for the party's nomination for president. On March 12, 1968, McCarthy won 42 percent of the vote in the New Hampshire primary; three weeks later, Johnson, perhaps understanding things would only continue to get worse, went on national television and told a stunned American public that he would not be running for re-election.

McCarthy, now the front-runner, soon faced stiff competition: Robert F. Kennedy, brother of the late president, former U.S. attorney general, and now the freshman senator from New York, was entering the race. Kennedy quickly became the front-runner, but on June 6, after winning the California primary (and presumably the nomination), he was shot and killed by Sirhan B. Sirhan, an immigrant from Jordan who objected to Kennedy's support for Israel as a Jewish homeland. The nomination ultimately went to Hubert H. Humphrey, Johnson's vice president; even as Humphrey was accepting the nomination at the Democratic convention in Chicago, Chicago police were doing battle with antiwar protesters outside.

The Republican nominee, former Vice President Richard M. Nixon, faced no such strife within his own party. Nixon, who had run for governor in California in 1962 and lost, had revived his career spectacularly and took to the campaign trail, telling voters he had a plan to end the war in Vietnam but never quite specifying exactly what that plan was. The final vote was tallied: George Wallace, the segregationist governor of Alabama representing the American Independent Party, got nearly 10 million votes; Humphrey got nearly 31 million; and Nixon got some 800,000 more. Richard Nixon, denied the presidency in 1960 and the governorship of Califor-

nia two years later, was now President of the United
States.

THIS, I NEED?: PART III

Nixon inherited the Vietnam War, but he was determined to avoid the same fate that had befallen Johnson.
Almost immediately, he began a program he called "Vi-
etnamization," or turning the war back over to the South
Vietnamese, by reducing the number of U.S. ground
troops in Vietnam, while increasing the bombing of the
enemy. He also sent troops into and started bombing
the neighboring countries of Laos and Cambodia, in an
attempt to check the spread of Communism and cut off
Vietcong supply lines (not exactly legal, but Nixon did
it all in secret). He dispatched Secretary of State Henry

Richard Nixon

Kissinger on a secret peace mission, and even traveled abroad himself to discuss the matter with major Communist powers. Still, the protests continued. On September 4, 1970, Ohio National Guardsmen fired upon a crowd of students protesting the war at Kent State University in Ohio, killing three. Nixon, under increasing pressure to end the war, signed the Paris Peace Treaty with North Vietnam in January 1973. The last U.S. troops left South Vietnam on April 30, 1975. Immediately, the country fell to the Communists—an event that, over the previous decade or so, nearly 60,000 U.S. soldiers, sailors, pilots, and marines had been killed attempting to prevent.

DÉTENTE, GLASNOST, PERESTROIKA, AND OTHER FOREIGN WORDS

Détente is a French for "a release from tension," or something like that. History, however, has chosen that word to name a trend in U.S.–Soviet relations that began in 1969, with a conference between the United States and the Soviet Union in Helsinki, Finland. The Strategic Arms Limitation Talks, or SALT, were a serious attempt to limit the production of nuclear weapons; but the process was slow, and it would be a year before the two superpowers would take even the first earnest step, signing a Nuclear Non-Proliferation Treaty sponsored by the United Nations.

The next step, though, was even bigger. In February 1972, Richard Nixon became the first U.S. president to visit the People's Republic of China, known to the West as "Red China." Nixon, who had begun his political career in 1946 by running for Congress as a fierce anti-communist, now undertook the task of making peace with one of the largest Communist nations in the world. The United States had had no diplomatic relations with China since 1949, when Mao Tse-tung and his Communist army had ousted the U.S. ally Chiang Kai-shek. Just before his visit, Nixon had called for the United States to begin trading with China as it did with other Communist nations; by the end of his visit, Nixon and Mao agreed that their countries should "normalize" relations. Before Nixon's visit, many Americans had considered such a statement inconceivable.

Three months later, Nixon became the first U.S. president to visit Moscow in peacetime. Nixon traveled to the Soviet capital to meet with Leonid Brezhnev, the secretary-general of the Soviet Communist Party (i.e., the top Russian honcho) to discuss improving trade relations and reducing their nuclear weapons arsenals. Just thirteen years earlier, Nixon, then vice president, had engaged Khruschev in a televised debate that more closely resembled a shouting match. Now Nixon was returning on a mission of peace. And he was pretty good at it, too. Before Nixon left, he and Brezhnev had signed seven agreements covering everything from trade to arms control to the exploration of outer space to a plan to defuse inadvertent military conflicts. Not long after Nixon's return, the Senate voted 88 to 2 to approve the SALT Treaty, limiting the number of nuclear missiles and submarines that each superpower would deploy.

Brezhnev visited the United States the following year, but after that the process of detente began to deteriorate slowly. In the mid-1970s, protesting the Soviet Union's treatment of Jews, Congress rejected several proposed trade agreements; the Soviets retaliated by rejecting pro-

Jimmy Carter

posed arms cuts. Then, in December 1979, the Soviet Union invaded neighboring Afghanistan. President James Earl "Jimmy" Carter objected strenuously, going so far as to boycott the summer 1980 Olympic Games in Moscow (the Soviets would retaliate by boycotting the summer 1984 Olympic Games in Los Angeles), but he did not intervene militarily. Carter's credibility—and the nation's prestige—suffered seriously when, just a month earlier, some 500 Iranian students stormed the United States embassy in Teheran and took sixty-six Americans hostage. Once again, Carter appeared powerless, and after a secret rescue mission ended in disaster, his presidency had become such an object of contempt and ridicule that, when he ran for re-election, he was easily defeated by his Republican opponent, Ronald Wilson Reagan the former California governor. Iran finally freed the hostages on January 20, 1981—the day Ronald

Reagan was inaugurated—after 444 days in captivity. The timing of this resolution has been used by pundits to attribute the release to Reagan's reputation as a hardline Cold Warrior, but in truth negotiations had been going on well before Reagan had even won the election.

Iranian hostages return home

Nevertheless, Reagan benefited immensely from the timing of the hostages' release, and he used the momentum to establish a hard-line policy with the Soviet Union that completely abandoned detente and swung closer to antagonism. Reagan referred to the Soviet Union as an "evil empire" in a speech, and committed the ultimate blooper when, preparing for a radio address, he leaned into the microphone and jokingly announced that he had declared the Soviet Union illegal and that the United States would commence bombing the Soviet

Union in five minutes. Unbeknownst to Reagan, the microphone was already on.

Ronald Reagan

Reagan subscribed to a policy of "peace through strength," which called for a massive defense buildup, including the extremely expensive Strategic Defense Initiative (SDI), nicknamed "Star Wars," a plan (never actually realized) to use satellites armed with lasers to protect the United States from missile attacks. Reagan also sent aid and military advisers to the anti-Communist government in El Salvador and anti-Communist Contra rebels in Nicaragua—possibly even after Congress voted to make such aid illegal. To finance these unprecedented expenditures, Reagan slashed or eliminated popular domestic programs—many of which benefited the poor, minorities, and the arts—and dramatically increased the federal budget deficit.

In March 1985, Mikhail Gorbachev became General Secretary of the Soviet Communist Party. At first, Gorbachev did not appear to be any different from his predecessors, aside from the fact that, at the age of fifty-four, he was about a generation younger. Gorbachev and Reagan met for a summit in Geneva, Switzerland, that November, but the two didn't agree on much except that they should meet again in the United States the following year. By 1987, though, it was becoming clear that Gorbachev was a different kind of Soviet leader. For one thing, he had embarked upon a policy of glasnost, a Russian word meaning "openness," or something like that; this meant that Soviet citizens were slowly gaining greater freedom of expression, including political expression. For another, he embarked upon a policy of perestroika, or "restructuring." He was in other words, reforming Soviet society, including the economy, from the ground up (or from the top down, depending on your perspective).

On December 8, 1987, Reagan and Gorbachev signed the Intermediate Nuclear Forces (INF) Treaty, in which they both agreed to destroy all of their own intermediate-range nuclear missiles. Gradually, Gorbechev loosened the Soviet Union's grip on other Communist nations in Eastern Europe, granting them greater—and eventually complete—autonomy, and withdrawing Soviet troops. By the end of 1989, Gorbachev had withdrawn the last Soviet troops from Afghanistan, and the Berlin Wall, the most notorious symbol of the east-west spilt in Europe, had fallen—literally. Soon, the Soviet Union itself ceased to exist, being split into a number of autonomous republics, each holding its own democratic elections. It is debatable whether this series of events can be attributed to Reagan's massive defense expenditures—which may have driven the Soviet Union to bankruptcy in an effort to keep up—or to Gorbachev's shrewd realization that Communism was failing and reforms were inevitable; debatable, and likely to be debated for years and decades to come. Only two things are certain: the third world war (the one that had never, officially, been declared, but had dragged on for more than four decades and had claimed hundreds of thousands of lives) was, at last, over, and the United States had clearly won.

Another undeclared war, though, was fought entirely within the United States, and it is hardly clear when—or even if—that war ended.

PART II: THE COLD CIVIL WAR

THE DECISION HEARD ROUND THE WORLD, OR AT LEAST THROUGHOUT THE SOUTH

On May 17, 1954, as the U.S. Army–McCarthy hearings were taking place in the Capitol, another, even more important historic moment was occurring nearby, in the Supreme Court. On that day, the Court ruled on the case of Linda Brown, a little girl who had sued the Board of Education of Topeka, Kansas, over its policy of racial segregation—maintaining "separate but equal" schools for whites and blacks. The Court ruled unanimously in favor of Miss Brown. In his decision, Chief Justice Earl Warren—the former Republican governor of California who had delivered the state for Eisenhower in the 1952 election—wrote:

> We conclude that in the field of public education the doctrine of "sepa-

Berlin Wall comes down

rate but equal" has no place. Separate educational facilities are inherently unequal.

Simple enough, right? Well, in 1954 those words hit certain parts of the country as hard as the Soviet Union's new atomic bombs. Racial segregation was still the law of the land in many states, most of them below the Mason-Dixon line, but not all. In these states, almost everything was segregated by race: restrooms, restaurants, water fountains, waiting rooms, buses, trains, public parks, even hospitals. But the most hallowed ground to the segregationist was the "whites-only" public school. It was absolutely imperative, according to this mindset, that white children never be forced, or even a*llowed*, to attend classes with black children.

In Chicago, though, the public schools had been integrated for many years, and that way of life was all fourteen-year-old Emmett Till had ever known. In August 1955, Till visited relatives in Money, Mississippi, and told them about his racially mixed school in Chicago. He even claimed to have a white girlfriend. To his Mississippi cousins and their friends, Till's claim was unbelievable; such a thing could never happen in Mississippi. Some of them dared Till to walk into a store and ask the white woman working there for a date. Till went into the store, bought something, and, as he was leaving, said, "Bye, Baby," to the woman, Carolyn Bryant (other accounts hold that he whistled at her, instead). Three days later, two white men (the woman's husband, Roy Bryant, and his half brother, J. W. Milam) kidnapped Till in the middle of the night, tortured him, shot him in the head, and threw his body into the Tallahatchie River. Bryant and Milam were arrested; reporters from all over the world attended the trial, which had become, to many, a referendum on the *Brown* decision and racial justice in the South. Despite overwhelming evidence of their guilt, though, the two defendants were acquitted by a jury of twelve white men, who had deliberated just long enough to have a snack.

Meanwhile, two civil rights leaders in Mississippi, the Reverend George W. Lee, in Belzoni, and Lamar D. Smith, in Brookhaven, were murdered, Smith having been shot in broad daylight on the steps of the Lincoln County Courthouse, where he was attempting to register black voters. No one was ever convicted of either crime. Despite the *Brown* decision, it was a bleak time

The arrest of Rosa Parks—Montgomery, Alabama 1955

for the Civil Rights Movement, which had begun after the Civil War and had gained great momentum after the Second World War, in which many African-Americans had fought overseas to crush the kind of racial bigotry and intolerance that they still faced at home.

Then, on November 25, 1955, the Interstate Commerce Commission abolished segregation on all interstate trains and buses, as well as in waiting rooms. A week later, on December 1, Rose Parks, a forty-three-year-old seamstress, was riding on a city bus in Montgomery, Alabama, when the driver ordered her to relinquish her seat to a white passenger. Parks refused; she had worked a long day and was too tired to stand. After a brief standoff, she was arrested, booked, and tossed in jail. Fortunately, Parks was a friend and erstwhile employee of E. D. Nixon, one-time head of the local branch of the National Association for the Advancement of Colored People (NAACP). Nixon posted bail for Parks and organized a one-day boycott of the Montgomery city buses to protest. The boycott—on Monday, December 5—was so successful that the participants decided to continue it until the city abandoned its policy of segregating buses. The boycotters chose, as their leader, the new minister of the Dexter Avenue Baptist Church, an unknown twenty-six-year-old from Atlanta named Martin Luther King, Jr. King and the Montgomery Improvement Association held nightly prayer meetings, organized carpools to drive boycotters to work, and created a support network for the boycott; the nearly empty city buses were losing a great deal of money, but the city's white leaders refused to back down.

Despite economic pressures (many protesters lost their jobs) and violence (including the bombing of E. D. Nix-

Martin Luther King Jr.

on's home), the boycotters held out, then, in December 1956, the Supreme Court ruled that segregation on buses was unconstitutional. It was the first successful large-scale antisegregation boycott in the South, and it would serve as the model for most of the nonviolent civil rights protests that would take place in the coming decade—at schools and stores, lunch counters, and college campuses. Many would end in violence—like the integration of the University of Mississippi in October 1962, when the arrival of African-American student James Meredith touched off a riot that left two people dead—and dozens of activists would lose their lives, most notably Medgar Evers, head of Mississippi's branch of the NAACP, who was shot in the back in his own driveway one night in June 1963. But the mainstream movement stood by its nonviolent ethos, earning the respect, admiration, and support of millions of Americans, black and white. On August 28, 1963, more than 200,000 of them gathered in Washington, D.C., to show their support for the movement and to hear Martin Luther King express his hopes for the future in his famous "I Have a Dream" speech. King, who was by then the nation's best-known civil rights leader and a symbol of the quest for racial equality and justice, would be awarded the Nobel Peace Prize the following year, but he would not live to see his dreams realized. Less than five years later, on April 4, 1968, he was assassinated in Memphis, Tennessee.

WHOLE LOTTA MOVEMENTS GOIN' ON

In 1964 and 1965, Congress passed legislation designed to secure civil rights—especially the right to vote—for all Americans, regardless of color. By the late 1960s, the "white-only" signs had, for the most part, been taken down from the restrooms and water fountains, and African-Americans no longer had to sit at the back of the bus. These battles—the obvious battles, the ones which engaged the hearts and sympathies of millions of previously unconcerned Americans—had been won. But other battles—like those against more subtle forms of discrimination, namely, in housing, bank lending, the workplace, and higher education—had yet to be fought, much less won.

Well before the assassination of Martin Luther King, the Civil Rights Movement had begun to splinter over some of these battles. Many African-Americans were growing impatient with the slow pace of desegregation;

some blamed King's policy of nonviolence. New factions began to emerge, groups that advocated a more confrontational approach; these were often lumped under the general name "black power," a phrase first uttered by Stokely Carmichael during a rally in Greenwood, Mississippi, in 1966. Black power was used by whites and the media to encompass all kinds of groups that in reality had very little in common (aside from a belief in the necessity of "black pride"). These groups included the Congress of Racial Equality (CORE), which advocated black separatism; to the Nation of Islam or "Black Muslims," whose most famous leader, Malcolm X (who was assassinated in 1965), advocated greater self-reliance for African-Americans; to the Black Panthers, who advocated a strategy of "picking up the gun." To exacerbate the situation, starting in 1964, riots swept through black neighborhoods in many major and mid-size U.S. cities.

When Richard Nixon was elected president in 1968, he promised, among other things, to restore "law and order." But Nixon himself was undone by the lawlessness of some of the top members of his administration who were implicated (along with Nixon himself) in a plot to break into the headquarters of the Democratic National Committee at the Watergate Hotel in Washington, and then another plot to impede the investigation of the crime. The Watergate scandal, as it is known, ultimately resulted in Nixon resigning from office on August 9, 1974, the first president to do so; but perhaps the greatest victim of the scandal was the presidency itself, which suffered a major loss of prestige from which many pundits believe it has never recovered.

Meanwhile, other groups, perhaps inspired by the successes of the Civil Rights Movement, were starting to agi-

Geraldine Ferraro runs for vice president

tate for their rights and the improvement of their circumstances. Hispanic-Americans working as migrant laborers in California joined the United Farm Workers, whose leader, Cesar Chavez, initiated a strike against the growers of table grapes in protest over low wages and deplorable working conditions; it would last for five years. In 1963, Betty Friedan published *The Feminine Mystique*, which challenged the righteousness and necessity of women's traditional domestic roles; the book is often cited as the inspiration for the modern feminist movement. On June 10, 1963, Congress passed the Equal Pay Act, guaranteeing that women would receive the same pay as men for doing the same work (although enforcing the act would, in years to come, prove difficult), and the 1964 Civil Rights Act extended to women the same protection against discrimination as it did to African-Americans; it also created the Equal Employment Opportunity Commission to enforce compliance. And in 1966, the National Organization for Women (NOW) was formed, with the objective of combating sexual discrimination.

Government backed its legislation with action; in 1981, President Reagan appointed Sandra Day O'Connor as the first female justice on the United States Supreme Court (Thurgood Marshall, the first African-American Supreme Court Justice, was appointed in 1967; as of 1998 no Hispanic-American or Asian-American had been appointed to the high court). The greatest leap for women's rights came in 1984, when Geraldine Ferraro, a congresswoman from New York, became the first woman nominated by a major party (the Democrats) to run for vice president of the United States. The 1992 elections, which sent a Democrat—William Jefferson "Bill" Clinton—to the White House for the first time in twelve years, sent more women to Congress than ever before. And in 1997, President Clinton appointed former U.N. ambassador Madeline Albright to be Secretary of State,

President William Jefferson Clinton

the highest position ever held by a woman in the United States Government.

Nevertheless, despite all of these advances, many believe that much of the progressive ground gained in the 1960s, and even earlier, was lost in the eighties and nineties. Whether that's true or not is open to dispute; but it is indisputable that the "civil cold war" is, at least on some fronts, still raging to this day.

SO, WHERE ARE WE, EXACTLY?

In a sense, the cold war and the Civil Rights Movement exemplify almost everything that has happened in America, and to Americans, since 1880. The cold war represents the most recent phase of a century that has seen the United States transformed from a relatively small, relatively isolated nation to what is unquestionably the greatest global power in the modern age; what will follow largely remains to be seen, but events like the 1991 Gulf War—in which the United States (under the leadership of president George Bush, Ronald Reagan's former Vice President) led an international coalition that drove invading Iraqi troops out of Kuwait—and brutal civil wars in the former Yugoslavia and Rwanda (both of which have required the intervention of peace-keeping U.S. troops) are strong indications that the end of the Cold War does not necessarily mean global peace.

The Civil Rights Movement represents an era when America was—and still is—attempting to live up to its reputation as a "great melting pot" that welcomes and incorporates and assimilates human beings from every country in the world, all the while struggling to overcome racial quandaries and crises that are as old—and, indeed, as American—as America itself.

If the process seems incomplete, that is because history itself is not a neat, clean-cut affair. Things don't always work out the way that we expect them to, or think they should; sometimes, they don't work out at all. But, to a large extent, whether or not history "works" at all is up to us. It is up to us to trace and track trends from the past to the present, up to us to decide what lessons we want to take from yesterday and apply to tomorrow. If there's one thing that we should have learned in studying America from 1880 to the present, it is that history is anything but a flat, fixed list of names, places, and dates. History is about stories that change a little bit every time a new generation tells them, about events that might be altered, in retrospect, with the revelation of new information, about mysteries that might never be solved. Most of all, history, especially the history of this country's last century or so, is about people—individual men and women, rich and poor, powerful and obscure— who did or wrote or said something that changed the way other people thought or acted or lived their lives. And we ourselves—every last one of us—are a part of it.